REMEMBER THE WITCH WITHIN

phoebe garnsworthy

CHAPTERS

Introduction	1
Your Inner Medicine Woman	10
My Inner Medicine Woman	12
Setting the Sacred Space	16

ALFRED
Alfred	24
Alfred II	36
Alfred Reflections	45

SELINA
Selina	55
Selina II	62
Selina Reflections	70

BONITA
Bonita	76
Bonita II	84

GABRIELLA
Gabriella	94
Gabriella Reflections	102

GEORGIANA
Georgiana	107
Georgiana II	116

REIKO

Reiko	128
Reiko II	136

MARGARET

Margaret	146
Margaret Reflections	157

The Power of Intention	163
Released and Me Again	167
Books by Phoebe Garnsworthy	174
About the Author	177

To the inner witch within all of us.
May your presence be free.
May your story be known.

Introduction

I trust that everything in my life happens for a reason, and that reason is to help me become the best version of myself. I invite creativity into my life as I explore my world with new eyes and new cycles of energy.

When inspiration strikes me, it does so like lightning. I feel as though an outside force erupts within me and itches to move through me. I allow that energy to be released through my fingertips. And, as I write these words for you as fast as I can, I feel an immense euphoric rush engulf my vision, allowing the energy from above to move through me. At this very moment, I am receiving an overload of information about the concept of this book as it comes to fruition. But, like all my books, I never really know exactly what's going to happen, or how the story will unfold. All I know is that I need to share it with you.

But where do I begin? Do I start with this lifetime or one of the lifetimes that led me to this point? Or, perhaps I start at the moment that everything changed....

All my life, I had been searching for a moment like this. I had been waiting for someone to tell me, "This is who you are, this is where you belong." And most importantly, "This is what you are meant to do in life." But of course, that never happened. I had to find out for myself. I had to learn what it meant to belong to my body, what it meant to respect and love the authenticity of my soul's voice. And even though it's my soul speaking through me clearly right now, my confidence trembles as I discover the truth of my being, while my heart rests with peace.

It started on my 36th birthday. I had purchased some books on witchcraft to read during a holiday in Portugal with my partner. I was, at a time in my life, finally owning my writing, and proudly calling myself an author. But in terms of my writing style or what I wrote and for whom, I wasn't sure. The words I spoke and wrote weren't taught to me; they were ideas I had acquired over many lifetimes; they were thoughts I had channeled through my soul. The advice I shared was based on my own spiritual practices—that I had created throughout my life or did without thinking. I had nurtured a connection with nature, with the elements of energy, but I never knew where they came from or how they came to be in me. I just did them.

I always followed my vivid imagination with the hope of finding answers to my many questions. I often practiced unusual rituals throughout my childhood. I would explain them to my friends as a game, yet they always had an esoteric theme behind them. Most often my "games" would be called "initiation rituals" because the friends who participated were always new, and I needed to initiate them into my circle. Although the games were indeed part of my eclectic imagination, there was something familiar and mechanical about the way I conducted them. I never questioned my actions, I just knew what came next.

I remember waking at 3 a.m. one night, walking outside to the bonfire that had burned down, taking the black ashes, and using them to create a spell of protection around the house. Where the practice came from, I didn't know, but I was able to perform it precisely with confidence and with no terror of the witching hour. I stood outside alone in the garden beneath the moonlight, despite being a small child of no more than 10 years old. That is just one memory I have of following my soul's mission without allowing my mind to interfere, but there are so many more.

I remember casting my first love spell at age 16, and having my high school crush, who was in no way interested in me, become my first-ever boyfriend. But most importantly, I have kept a sacred altar throughout my life, and if you've read my other books— specifically *Align with Soul*—you would know about how important this altar was for me when harnessing the energies of the universe. But again, I had no idea why I collected these items, nor the true power they possessed; they just made me happy. And like everything in life, we need to move closer to the things that light up our souls.

But as I got older, and began to recognize my friend's awkwardness when I suggested they partake in magical games, or exhibited my peculiar fascination with the spiritual realm, I realized it would be best to keep my desires hidden. Although I continued to create and practice rituals on my own, it wasn't until my early 30s that I recognized the importance of sharing my authentic self, and I finally allowed those passions to breathe again in public.

But here, today, on my 36th birthday, as I read about the traditions of witchcraft, I see those words as though I had once written, lived, and breathed them.

Over the next 12 hours, a great download of information took place as the story of my past unraveled before me. All the things I had done as a child didn't seem so weird anymore; instead, I looked at them with admiration. I was proud of myself for acting upon my soul's calling without questioning its absurdity, and pursuing my passions without fear. And for the first time in my life, I felt a true connection; I felt like I had revealed the core of my origin. But there was something deep within that was holding me back from truly aligning with it. There was a great hesitation gripping my heart. It wouldn't let me move forward freely. As I further examined the religion of Paganism, and the many tiers of worship that came beneath it—such as witchcraft, druidism, and folklore—I found many areas that I resonated with deeply. But most importantly, I found the same beliefs on self-reliance, self-empowerment, and connection with the spirit world that I had been practicing throughout my life. The unstinting of these ideas and concepts came more naturally to me than any form of education I had ever received. Still, I was stuck. Despite the undoubtable connection I felt with witchcraft, I still couldn't bring myself to say that I am a witch. And it wasn't because I didn't believe that I was one, I just wasn't able to truly own the title. There was something holding me back from stepping into my power. I didn't hold the confidence. Furthermore, I associated the word—witch—with something bad. But why?

I continued to explore my hesitation, by following a string of questions, like I do with any form of limiting belief. I followed that invisible thread back through my life, searching for its origin, desperate to find out why I felt the need to conceal my power. When I followed that string of questions I arrived at the beginning of my life, but the web continued beyond that. Then I realized, that string of questions, of limiting beliefs, of fear of who I was, had existed in many lives before my current one, and in many of my ancestors' lives. I knew that if I wanted to heal that fear for myself and my future children, I needed to delve deep into those lives and find out what happened and why. And hopefully, here, I will find my power again.

And this is how I came to write this book—through a need to reveal both the truth about all the past lives that came before this one, what their connection to witchcraft was, and how to learn from those experiences.

But how do I do that? There's no evidence of who they were. There's no concrete information to say this is what they went through.

The idea of an afterlife is foreign for many who believe that this is our one and only life. So I needed to find a way to explore with great trust. I had explored past life regressions several times through hypnosis with the help of an advisor. I'd had incredible results, so I knew what it meant and how it felt to explore past life energy. But to write this book, I wanted to do it myself. My meditative journeys have always been extremely visual, and I have been practicing for many years to meet my spirit guides through these mediums. I have sought out wisdom, counsel, and guidance through my spiritual practices, and I have never been let down or led astray. So, for this book, I followed the same connection with the spirit world, but instead of asking questions about the present or the future, I simply changed my intention to explore the energy of the past. Through the combination of self-hypnosis, meditation, and a witchcraft ritual, I was able to create my own transcendental journey to explore my past selves, my past lives, and those of my ancestors.

When we journey, our soul travels through an opening of space-time energetic vibration. We can understand this concept by looking to the theory that everything is energy, and energy never dies. So the energy that was created once upon a time by people who lived before us is still available for us to access. Perhaps in the time that has passed, that energy has transformed (most likely), but we can still call upon it. It can still transform back to show us that period of life. Because memory is not local—it isn't contained in our brain. So, if memory is an energy, it can be accessed beyond the physical.

When we journey within the spirit world, there are no secrets; we simply ask and we are told. Inside each journey, I was presented with vivid images that told their story. Sometimes the images ignited with fine detail translating the knowledge easily. Other times, I needed to work a little harder to understand what the message was. My strongest telepathic qualities have always been visual. Second to this is feeling—I can *sense* what is known, what is told and what is felt. I can embody the emotions. And lastly, I hear the words. I hear them subtly, not from the voice of the person, but from the voice of my own inner knowing. That inner voice is the hardest one for us to trust—for our mind likes to challenge and take control—but with diligent practice, we can learn to distinguish between the voice in our head and that of our soul.

What you need to remember when traveling to these outer realms, is that what you see may be a representation of your own memories in this life. Because what you see in the spirit realm are visual projections of energy. Our mind likes to form definitions in order to understand. When receiving information, it will usually identify the concept as something it already knows to be able to reference it appropriately. So, as I journeyed through different lands and times, and met the people, many of them were presented as lifelike characters I had seen as a child. Now, the question still remains, did what I see as a child really happen, or was I tapping into unconscious energy? For, as children, we do not have the same veils of illusion that we have as adults. Regardless of what was seen, what matters most is the message and this is what I captured from each of my ancestors and my past lives.

If I ran out of time with one character, I would call out to it again when entering my trancelike state at a later date. Hence, fleshing out the gaps in their story. The following stories were "remembered" over a period of several months and many journeys.

Every chapter, every character, every life represented in this book, I have learned about from inner world journeys. They are all unique—each with their own wisdom and message. Through these stories, I learned about my own story. Through these lives, I understand my own. This exploration of my past provided me with the answers I had been seeking since a very young age. I can finally understand why I was cautious to explore the spiritual side of myself, and to share those explorations through my writing.

I hope this book will encourage you to explore your own past, your connections to your ancestors, and recognize how they shaped you, for better or worse. We are all holding onto ancestral trauma. The more we explore and share what happened to us, to our ancestors, to our community, the greater contribution we can make to healing the entire collective consciousness.

This is our story.

Your Inner Medicine Woman

Your *medicine* is your unique gift that can help heal the world. We each have a profound gift within us to share during our lifetime. And each of our gifts will assist the world in the transformation toward a better future for the next generation. We use the word *medicine* to define what your gift entails. Your gift, your medicine, is a form of healing that supports the entire conscious collective.

To find your gift can be your life's work. For it doesn't always present itself easily or clearly, and it can take much trial and error to unearth it. Sometimes people know what their gift is immediately, and they confidently share it. Whether you already know or you have to search for it, it doesn't matter. For every one of us will share our gift at some point in our lives. Whether it happens at the beginning or the end is irrelevant, for it's the process of our soul's evolution that is important. When your soul has evolved to a certain degree, then your medicine will become clear, and your life path and life purpose will be laid out with complete precision.

One day I decided to journey to the spirit realms to meet my inner Medicine Woman. I had an idea of who she was, of what the truth of my gift entailed, but I needed confirmation. My biggest weakness was a lack of confidence in my writing, and although I heard the calling from my soul that this was my destiny, my mind held tightly to fear; I could hear the voice of limiting beliefs, of inadequacy and ugliness. I wanted a sign so badly to find my path. To know that what I believed was true. I finally received the sign I was craving in my journey to the upper world. I was able to connect with my inner Medicine Woman and seek her wisdom. Little did I know that through this meeting, I would be able to reveal the truth of other wisdom, and learn why I had such a hard time believing in my own gift.

And so I journeyed.... This is my story.

My Inner Medicine Woman

My inner Medicine Woman is beautiful. She is the ultimate creator of all magic, miracles and life. She plays between the worlds of the seen and unseen. She thrives in nature, especially when surrounded by water, trees and sunlight. She loves the sound of waterfalls, and spends most of her time immersed in the lush green rainforest. She wears a long white dress and adorns her hair with sweet perfumed flowers. She is graceful, and elegant, a goddess of the highest vibration. Her goal is to create beauty wherever she goes.

She loves to play with magic, and fairies and the mystical creatures that surround her. Her life purpose is to spread joy and pleasure with a curious mind and open heart. She views life as fun, as an experiment, a game. If you are sad she will take away your pain with her hand on your heart, and replace that grief with love and laughter. She will bring forth the divine light within you, and remind you to honor and share this love with all who surround you. She is both blissful and blessed. She is a feminine warrior with a masculine balance, and embodies an unshakable strength of inner peace.

She comes from a long line of powerful women, of spiritual witches and pagan masters, who have carefully passed on their ancestral wisdom. She wanted to show me these women, for they are a part of my blood lineage, and so, together we explored the lives of my current ancestors.

My oldest ancestor lived thousands of years ago. She was an ancient tribal elder, a centenarian with beautiful dark wrinkled skin. She sat poised at a fire as the young children sat around and listened eagerly to her stories. She healed wounds through storytelling, and passed on wisdom from those who came before her. She told the children of how they came to Earth, about how they were both the created and the creator. And, because of her kindness and care for all creatures, she was adored and loved by all.

The next ancestor I met was part of an Asian tribe. She learned from the land, and listened to its wisdom. She was a great mother to her people and nurtured all who walked alongside her. With healing words, she blessed those around her; and with plant medicines, she soothed troubled souls. Her sacred teachings were shared and passed on to many women, and, as they evolved, their power grew too.

The ancestor I met after her was born at the beginning of the Middle Ages; here she ran her own apothecary.

She was a witch doctor who healed the sick and saved lives. She was greatly honored in the village. But the story of our wisdom being passed on through our ancestors stopped there, for she was the last who was allowed to use her gifts of knowledge from the spirit world.

Over the next few minutes, many visions played out, showing me how our divine feminine power was suppressed by the leaders who felt threatened. And I watched in agony as the women who did not conform to the male hierarchy system were hunted, tortured, and killed.

My ancestors learned how to hide their craft in order to survive. Many years passed, many lives, many wars, and the true story of their magic has now been forgotten. As I learned this truth, I realized that it explained my fear of owning my gifts and why connecting with the spirit world felt like a burden— I had been so used to concealing this connection for so long.

But now, in this life, the Medicine Women are remembering their magic. Each is believing in herself as her confidence grows. As she channels her inner world and the outer realms, she remembers the sacred rituals engraved on her heart. She remembers the spells that her tongue can create from authentically living her truth. And just like her eldest ancestor, she too is sharing great ancient wisdom through her stories. The ones who came before us will not have died in vain. They will be remembered.

We will remember the witch within us.

Setting the Sacred Space

Before every ritual, I like to take time to settle my energy in my sacred space. I do this by sitting in meditation for several minutes, calling out to the energy of my soul to come back into my body as I ground myself on Earth. Although my soul is going to be traveling through the cosmic realm to explore these past lives and the lives of my ancestors, it's important for me to remember that I am living *this* life. That I am here, in this moment, living a spiritual life in my body. It may sound silly, but it's just another layer of protecting one's energy. I remind myself that energy never dies, it simply transforms; and even though there is nothing to be feared about exploring different energies and those energies, it's important to protect and cleanse our energy often. This is how we will continue to live our lives with brilliance. When I sit in my meditation, this is what I am doing. I am gathering my energy, I'm cleansing and protecting it.

I sit in my meditation for as long as I need to feel good about myself. Because of my daily practice, I find that I can reach this stage of complete bliss at around 10 minutes, although this time frame can vary. Once I have entered this state of my own nirvana, I may choose to indulge in this energy longer, (if I desire more love); otherwise, I move swiftly onto my ritual and journey.

I define the space around me by tracing my finger along the edges of a beautiful antique cloth that belonged to my grandfather. I have been using this cloth since I was a child as it holds significant meaning to me. Sometimes I use my crystals to define the space, by placing them around me in a crystal grid. Other times, I simply use my hands, circling the space where I sit to clearly outline where I will be igniting my ritual. But to journey into my past lives, I will use my ancestors' cloth, for I wish for their blessings.

When I feel ready, I sit on the piece of colored fabric and assemble my ritual objects around me. This signifies that the ritual has commenced, for I have already taken the first step by defining the space. From here, I speak my intention out loud and ignite the second step of my ritual.

My intention has always been the same with each journey that I take to visit these lives. At times I ask for specific guidance about a particular life. And for some of those lives, I venture into the unseen realms multiple times to gather information. But each time, the core of the intention is the same: to learn what I needed to know about my heritage, about my past lives, about who I am and why I am here.

I repeat my intention several times in my mind as I continue to set up my sacred space and begin to call in the energies. Next, I ignite a strong connection between myself and the spirit realm, and I call out to my soul to guide me through the process. Although the core of my ritual is the same, I change it as I feel the need to. Like everything in life, we cannot be rigid with our repetition; change is what keeps our creativity blossoming.

Since I was small I have always created an area in my home where I could honor my soul on a daily basis. I call this my sacred altar. I would decorate that space to reflect my soul's desires. Over time that space changed, as the pieces that my soul adored changed, but they always held some connection with the Universal Energies. And as my awareness for what I was partaking in deepened, I found myself resorting back to the chief components of the Universal Energies of Earth, Air, Water, Fire and Spirit. My ritual space consists of tangible objects to represent these energies, and I connect with them as I call out to each of the energies to support me in the following way:

I call upon the energy of Fire, brilliant flames of transformation. May your pillars of strength protect my energy and illuminate the pathway before me so that I may journey to the unseen realms with safety and courage.

I call upon the energy of Water, fluid motion of resilience and beauty. May your soft presence harmonize my emotions so that I may enter these past and ancestral lives without attachment or fear.

I call upon the energy of Earth, great nurturing love from Mother Nature. May your blessings keep my energy grounded as I journey to the unseen realms to harness the wisdom of my ancestors and past lives.

I call upon the energy of Air, lightness of being, creator of change. May your clear vibrations keep my mind and heart open to receive the blessings of my ancestors and past lives, so that I may reveal the truth that I seek.

And I call upon the energy of Spirit, source of creation and curious light beings who pass my way. Come forth and guide me on my path, to heed this unique perception of history, so that I may bring forth the wisdom and clarity I need.

I speak my intention once more.

I am journeying to the unseen realms to reveal the truth of my ancestors and past lives that have helped shape my life.

I close my eyes and lie down, allowing my breath to ease. I can feel the energies swirling around me, they are gathering strength and transforming above my body as they merge to reveal a vortex point of exploration. It is the place of entry, a portal that is inviting my departure. My breath eases as I pick up my drum, and I begin to strum a soft humming beat to replicate the sound of my heart. I speak my intention clearly once more as I commence my journey into the angelic realm of unconsciousness.

The beat of my drum echoes in my ears as I see myself separate from my body. I am walking along a pathway of nothingness, awaiting the next steps that will pull me either above or below. A golden staircase appears before me, a signal that the upper world is calling my presence. As I choose to accept their invitation, I feel a sensation take hold and draw me closer to the upper realm.

I walk up the stairs effortlessly, but they appear different from how I had seen them in previous journeys. Usually, they appear as a simple gold ascending staircase, but here, I see a blue tinge of reflection over them, the effect of a soft, unusual texture upon the surface. There are no sharp defining edges, instead, the staircase is curved and fluid. And as I reach the top, the sound of rushing water fills my ears. When I walk closer, I can see that the platform edges of the upper world are covered with a thin layer of water overflowing the sides of the staircase, creating large waterfalls pouring from the heavens to the Earth.

As I stood on the platform surrounded by flowing water, a king and queen appeared straight ahead of me, dressed in blue royal robes. I walked over and kneeled before them.

"Who are you?" I ask.

"We are the gatekeepers. This is the kingdom of the past. We will advise you with any questions you may have," the queen replies.

"May I have your permission to write this book?" I ask them both solemnly, wondering what kind of response I would get. "Do I have your permission to journey to my past lives, and into the lives of my ancestors, to learn about the wisdom and history that has been carried over into my life? To understand the magic that resides within me and to realize what it is that I need to know?"

"You have my blessing." The king replies first. He nods warmly, and with his thumb, runs a line down my forehead toward my nose to symbolize his approval.

"Thank you," I say. I kiss his feet and bow.

Then I turned to the queen and awaited her response. She sat with a child in her womb, and an incredible vision of beauty and confidence emanated from her.

Her crown is fastened with clear quartz. She smiles and repeats the same gesture as the king, crossing my forehead with her thumb.

"Thank you," I say as I kiss her feet and bow.

"The pathway on your right will lead you to the lives of your ancestors, and on your left, you will enter the lives of your own past." the king says, as two misty pathways appear before us. "The choice is yours."

I look at each pathway and open up my energy to be drawn to either side. I immediately feel a strong pull from the right, beckoning me toward my ancestors. I promptly follow, waving goodbye to the king and queen. The moment my foot steps onto the path it turns into a downward slope. I feel something at the bottom quickly take hold of my energy and pull me down. Despite the hurried nature and unknown adventure ahead of me, there is no fear within me. I just know, wherever I go, is where I need to be.

Alfred

Alfred

I arrived at an old wooden door in the middle of a small village. It was nighttime, and only the soft flickers of moonlight lit the way. The village consisted of a few mud houses lining a narrow dirt road, and it reminded me of the Middle Ages. Which, according to my inner Medicine Woman journey, would mean that I hadn't arrived at my oldest ancestor, but instead, I had arrived right in the middle of my ancestry bloodline.

I stood there for several minutes gaining awareness by defining my surroundings. I knew from my previous visions in the spirit world that the longer I spent articulating the layout, the deeper I was able to journey into it. So, I focused my attention between the dimly lit street, the village, and the wooden door. When I felt like I had stabilized my connection, I knocked on the door with immense curiosity, wondering what my intention could bring.

The door swung open instantly. In front of me was a woman around 70 years old with a toothy grin. She was slightly hunched over, with round cushiony cheeks, and spikes of gray hair popping out from under her bonnet.

"Come in," she said, waving me through and smiling cheerily. It seemed as though she had been waiting for me. "I'm Alfred."

Alfred wore a forest green dress covered by a white apron and stood at a shabby wooden table in the middle of the room. I was mesmerized by the room. The walls were decorated from floor to ceiling with small jars containing different herbs and spices. I was utterly overwhelmed by the variety of scents emitting from the jars; I longed to open each one and ask what they were used for. It was a giant apothecary of herbs and spices, with the knowledge of how to create them into magic. Everything I had ever wanted. I had been exploring the powers of plant medicines in my waking life, and I knew that we could make endless combinations from just a few simple herbs to heal ourselves. Before I could ask the woman any questions, she interrupted my thoughts.

"Come in, come in, I told you. We haven't much time." Alfred quickly ushered me through the door, locking it securely behind her. "They'll be here soon," she whispered.

Alfred paced around the kitchen, taking a jar from the wall and pouring out some crushed leaves into the bowl before her. She started mixing its content quickly with a spoon, all the while looking at the door behind me, waiting for someone to come through it.

I felt a tightening in my chest and the mist of stressful energy in the air. As I took a deep breath, I tried to settle myself; I reminded myself that this was just a journey. But I felt scared. I felt like there was something happening beyond my control and that Alfred's safety was threatened.

When you journey into past lives you are tapping into the energy that was created back then. Although it doesn't actually affect you now, it can physically feel very real, like you are reliving those emotions and experiences. The energy translates instantly. Often, when it's our own trauma we've created, we have the power to heal those emotions when we feel them again. Like any form of healing, we need to move through that energy and let it rest. But because this wasn't my own past life but that of my bloodline, all I could do was witness, to hear the story, and help heal it. That was how I felt as I watched Alfred. As I pried into her life, I found there was something stressful about it. The energy of this period was startling me, and I felt as though I had to walk carefully. So, I slowed my breathing down, trying not to make a sound.

"Who's they?" I whispered.

"I can't say their names," Alfred replied quietly, wiping her hands on her apron and rushing back to the door. "They're bringing me another soldier to heal." She continued, as she pressed her ear against the door to listen. "No one can see them coming or we'll all be killed."

Alfred looked to me as she listened at the door. But there was no pity in her face. I felt her strength. Despite the challenge she was faced with, she had warrior blood in her veins and she carried on calmly, with a sense of urgency. She wasn't flustered. She moved about the space with order, with precision. Although her face was full of wrinkles, and she appeared to be quite fragile and withered, her energy felt vibrant. Her mind was sharp. And the compassion in her heart to help others was overflowing.

"I never used to live like this," Alfred said as she walked back over to the kitchen bench and continued to make a potion. "There was once a time when my gifts were valued. When being a healer was respected and honored by everyone." She continued, as her eyes lit up with pride. "People used to travel many days to come see me... but that was before. Now look at me. Always looking over my shoulder. Always by myself, working in secret. I can trust no one. They're giving money to people who tattle on us. They're trying to smoke us out one by one."

Alfred poured the contents of the potion into a tiny glass bottle and walked over to a large clay pot that sat by the door. She lifted the cloth that covered it and placed the potion inside. She picked up another potion in a bottle and carefully rotated it, lifting it up toward the light from the candle and studying its contents carefully before placing it back in the clay pot. Then she returned to her space behind the kitchen counter.

The scene repeated itself. Alfred would gather some herbs from the jars on the wall, mix them together in the bowl and turn them into a potion. All the while, rushing back and listening at the door, waiting for something to happen. I stirred in my journey slightly, wanting it to move forward. So I set my intention again. *Show me what I need to know. Tell me more about your life.* I asked, to which a vision of Alfred as a small child swept through my mind.

I saw Alfred as a young girl, up high on her tiptoes, reaching for the powders on the shelves, pointing to them and reciting their name and properties by memory. Alfred's fascination with the spirit realm was a natural calling from her soul. To inherit the wisdom of the universe was an organic desire for her. The story of her life was told to me quite simply. Alfred's parents and her grandparents, and her grandparents' parents, and their parents, were all extremely powerful witch doctors. They held the greatest knowledge of alchemy and apothecary ever to exist. Their knowledge had been accumulated from their long line of ancestors, and from their many travels to meet with other renowned witch doctors around the world. Seeking guidance from the spirits through divination and high ritual magic was their greatest achievement, and they had mastered this connection over centuries. To create herbal potions and incantations was a natural occurrence in their work, and they took on the role as some of the greatest healers in all of the land. They didn't just cure incurable diseases with plant medicines and spells, they also provided emotional and mental support as well, reminding the patients of their own divinity and their ability to create the change they sought.

I then saw a vision of Alfred in her early twenties, giving advice to the regional king and queen. Alfred stood in the bed chambers of the queen, using solely her hands and voice to heal and support the queen so that she could give birth to a baby. After over fifteen years of trying, the queen had still not successfully carried a baby to term. Alfred visited the queen daily for two months, creating herbal concoctions and igniting sacred rituals. Alfred connected to the spirits and listened to their advice on how to heal the queen's womb. Within one year, the queen gave birth to a healthy baby boy. All thanks to Alfred. But that was one of her last memories of success. For shortly after the kingdom was overtaken by the neighboring countries, and the empire was demolished. Alfred's magical past and healing hands were no longer looked upon as a great miracle; the power she possessed and the support she received from the townsfolk made her appear as a threat to the sovereign.

"And now they want to erase our story," Alfred said, bringing my attention back to where she was standing in the kitchen as she continued to create her potions. "They're burning our papers and destroying our temples. Any art or statues that we once praised have been abandoned or buried. If we dare to be ourselves we'll be punished by death."

"And were you... eventually...?" I didn't have the heart to finish the sentence, to ask if she was caught. I hated the thought of her being killed in such a brutal fashion. A part of me was nervous that I would start crying in the middle of the journey. The other half would have been angry that such a tragedy could've taken place. Even though I knew how delicate the life span was during this period of time, it amazed me that she had lived to be as old as she was.

"No, no, sweet child. I lived a long and happy life. Well for most of it." She nodded, raising her eyebrows. "But I was the last of our kind to live. You know. Truly live. Live openly in speaking our praises to the spirits. Live

REMEMBER THE WITCH WITHIN

with the feeling of freedom to be who we choose to be. I was the last to hold our ancestors' wisdom. All the rituals, all the magic, all the spells that our family worked hard to learn were all within me. So, when I passed, it passed too."

I felt my energy drawn to Alfred as she talked of magic and incantations and created the bottles of potions before me. I wanted so badly to soak up all of her wisdom. My thirst for exploration and educating myself was ripe and eager. But my desire to learn was overtaken by the question of why. *Why wasn't I given the chance to learn this from my own grandparents? Why were you forced into hiding? What happened to all of the wealth of knowledge that existed?* My mind wanted to take control and force my soul to take a back seat.

"And so you never had children to whom you could pass this knowledge?"

"I had one," Alfred replied as she pointed to the corner of the room where a young girl appeared before me. She sat in the corner with a dirty face and a sour look, rocking back and forth.

"She has the same gifts as me, my daughter, Bonita." Alfred looked to her as she spoke quietly so that her daughter couldn't hear. "But, she grew up to be too scared to use them. By the time Bonita was born, too many had died, and we could only practice our rituals in complete secret."

"So, she could never be true to herself?" I asked, looking at Bonita in the corner, but as I did, her image slowly faded away, stopping me from truly connecting with her.

I resonated with Bonita's fear of not being true to herself. The hesitation I had about not stepping into my true self haunted me throughout my life. I knew that I could live confidently as my authentic self, but I didn't believe in my own power to do so, and it was the easy option to side with fear. Yet, here I was, having seen a timid girl who didn't even have the opportunity to be her true self because she would be killed for doing so. How could I even compare myself! I was so lucky to be living in the world during a time when uniqueness was finally beginning to be celebrated and honored. I was voluntarily choosing not to seek confidence in my gifts, whereas Bonita wasn't even given the option. And even though I was faced with such tragedy before me, it gave me ammunition to step closer to my power. For it reminded me that at least I had a choice.

"Yes, she was never given the chance to be true to herself," Alfred replied.

Was she feeding my words to me, or was she an extension of my own thought process? I wondered. Here I was journeying with vibrant imagery before me, with great trust, for through belief was the only way I could understand. We need to just believe in our truth and act according to the feelings inside from our soul. Not to question it, but to simply feel our way forward. I nodded to Alfred, feeling myself trust her voice as that of my own grandparents, and I waited for her to explain more.

"The leaders were too powerful by the time Bonita grew up and we were forced into hiding. Not in the way that you think they did. Not in the way they wrote about us in your history books. But they forced us to turn on one another. They used fear to separate the communities. We used to be united together in the village. But then greed and jealousy made people turn on one another. We once had power but then they wanted it."

"We?"

"We, the women," she replied, narrowing her gaze toward me and staring at me intently. "We, the witches," she whispered, now looking over my shoulder and walking back to the door.

"We, the divine feminine who gives birth to creation." I heard a voice echo in my ears as an image of an angel-like woman flashed before me.

I felt the energy of the divine female overtake my senses. No longer was I holding that fearful stress that was ripe in the air. Now I was siding with comfort, with peace. I felt the strength of the collective. In this moment it was as though a choir of angels was singing sweet songs above me, calling out to me and sending me love.

"It still exists," Alfred replied, hearing my thoughts. "They tried to burn us. They tried to destroy our statues and bury our books and kill our passion. But the passion we hold with the spirit world is energy. And you can't destroy energy. That energy lives on. That energy lives on in you even if you don't realize it. The wisdom you seek is just hovering above your head, waiting to be harnessed."

A spider web of electric energy interwove above us now and it flickered with vibrating pulsations. To me, it symbolized the collective consciousness and the web of information that gathers and connects us. I felt as though I was being shown a pathway to remembering this truth before me. And that pathway involved exploring the seed of life's sacred geometry that was always available to me, I just forgot how to enter that particular frequency. And here was Alfred reminding me that all I needed to do was reach up and grab it. To reach up and hold it, to harness it and receive it. That wisdom had always been there, waiting for each of us to take it. It will never run out, it will only multiply and magnify with each energy that connects with it. I just needed to be brave enough to listen to what it said.

Alfred pressed her ear against the door and closed her eyes, listening intently. Then she lifted the wooden latch that had fastened the door, and opened it.

She turned and looked at me. "They're here."

Alfred II

Two men stood at the entrance with an unconscious man who appeared to be injured.

"Quick, over there," Alfred said, pointing to the corner where a sheet was hanging.

The men carried the injured man to the corner and placed him behind the sheet. They returned to Alfred, handed her a few coins, exchanged some words and left. Alfred locked the door quickly behind them. She walked behind the sheet to study the man, and then returned to making her potions on the wooden bench.

"It's to heal the inflammation," she said, as she crushed some herbs and spices to make a fine powder. "Rosemary, black pepper and turmeric." Then she squeezed juice from what appeared to be an aloe vera plant into the bowl to create a thick paste.

Alfred took the bowl and walked behind the sheet. I followed her. It felt like she wanted to show me. The injured man was lying on the floor with rags beneath his head and a fowl-smelling stench coming from his body. I couldn't see it clearly in my vision, perhaps it was my own mind trying to protect me, as I never could handle the sight of blood. I knew there was a terrible trauma on his leg, for Alfred started to apply the thick paste over it. The man shuddered with both pain and relief, yet continued to lie quite sound asleep. Alfred placed a cloth over his eyes and picked up a small sponge and bucket next to the bed. She started to clean his skin. I tried not to look at the man, but I felt drawn to. He was just lying there, so helplessly. And although I didn't know this man, nor what brought about his injury, to me he symbolized the many men who had gone to war and had their lives changed forever.

Both of my grandfathers had participated in World War II. And even though they had never shared stories, and no other family member spoke about it, we all knew war had changed them in ways we couldn't understand.

We all know that war is bad. One cannot truly comprehend what it must have felt like to be forced into war. The mentality required to break another human being's spirit is unfathomable. The reason for doing so is usually to fuel someone's greed. It will never be right. The aftermath of such a trauma can haunt a person throughout their whole life, and even those of subsequent generations. So many people suffer from post-traumatic stress disorder; so many people are unable to forget the images they saw or what they went through. It's difficult to see that anything positive comes from war, other than the miracle of survival, and continuation of the bloodline.

Yet, here I was in my ancestors' life, faced with a war-torn victim from hundreds of years ago. Still feeling the energy of fear, hate, distress and agony lingering in the air, I couldn't help but think that this energy was carried through the bloodline too. Most trauma is not likely healed properly, since we historically don't talk about these things. So, we, the children of people who lived during those difficult times are still holding onto some version of the pain that was created back then. There is so much more to heal than we know.

"Yes, this is how it all began," Alfred said as she threw the cloth back into the bucket and twisted the water out. "This is the moment we gave up our power. It all started with some kind of war, and a need for control."

Alfred closed her eyes and placed her hands just above the injured man's body. A low-pitched hum exited her lips as I stood there watching, mesmerized by her actions. Her hands softly caressed the space above his body as she gradually moved the energy down to his feet. I felt an immediate sense of peace wash over me, and a deep calling from within to learn more about this practice in my waking life.

At this moment, I recognized who Alfred resembled in the ancestral line of my Medicine Woman dreaming journey. She was the one who helped others in secret, she was the one whose wisdom of magic and connection with the energies of the universe was the most potent.

"I was the one." Alfred nodded, confirming my recognition. "And you will be the one who remembers."

"But, how?" I asked, admiring Alfred's power and her ability to be herself with such confidence. There was not an ounce of fear within her eyes; she wasn't troubled by what she saw, she just faced the challenge and solved it without question.

"By doing what you are doing right now. By learning about what we went through. When you look through my eyes with compassion and understanding at the reasons why we made the choices we made, you will view the past in a different light; you will see what needs to be done. You will heal this trauma."

"By understanding our world with deeper compassion, we will heal," I affirmed.

But just how difficult would it be to reveal the truth of what my ancestors went through?

Alfred walked back to the kitchen to allow the man to rest in peace. I swiftly followed her. She commenced her ritual of creating potions once more. Opening jars, pulling out spices and herbs, and mixing them in containers. Adding oils and sweet-smelling perfumes to her creations.

I looked at Alfred, reflecting upon her space and all that she was doing. She held a wealth of knowledge, there was no doubt about that. When I looked at her face, I could feel the ageless wisdom that she had accumulated, from the outer realms, from many ancestors and many lifetimes. And I wanted to learn. I was eager to heed that wisdom and feel the strength of her perception of the unknown. She had such a powerful presence, not of beauty, but of peace, and the energy she radiated oozed the power of freedom.

"What am I to learn from you?" I asked, approaching her workspace.

"By understanding what I see when I look at you and every living creature. I see you as the true spirit you are," Alfred said, as she picked up some dried leaves and crushed them into a fine powder using a mortar and pestle. "I do not see flesh, bones and blood, I see energy, I see vibration, I see your soul. I have always been right here dancing between worlds, but I walk in the unseen just as much as I walk in the physical

REMEMBER THE WITCH WITHIN

world. I see past the exteriors of our Earthly beings and deep into the magic of the universe. This knowledge is what will bring together the unity we seek. The more we learn about the power within us, and crumble the masks we show to the world, the closer we will be to transforming the entire conscious collective."

Alfred's words landed in my ears with great resonance. There was a strange familiarity with her manner, but I couldn't figure out whether I knew a version of her in my waking life. Often, we meet with our soul family in many lives, and sometimes in journeys, we can see who they are in our current lives. But with Alfred, I held no recognition of who she was in my current life; but her energy reminded me of that of my grandparents and I felt a sense of great respect for her.

"Let me show you." Alfred pinched the powdered leaves in her hand, lifted it up high and forcefully blew into it.

The powder floated up to the ceiling, where a hole opened up. Here, the powdered leaves transformed into floating dust. But instead of falling down as expected, it continued to fly. I followed it as Alfred instructed me to. The next thing I knew, I was also up high in the galaxy, following the dust that had now turned into sparkling stars. Alfred was next to me, giggling. The strange part was that we were not floating nor flying, we were simply connected and immersed in divinity, and supported by the energy of the universe.

Alfred pointed to the frame of our bodies, which immediately evaporated, and we floated together as shining lights of energy. The mirage of tangible existence reflected back and forth as she emphasized her point, showing me that her life-like mass was interchangeable with her desired vision, all the while holding its truth of divine loving bliss. It was an image she was choosing to show me. It reflected the metaphor that we choose our life to be how we make it. This was how we created our perception of the world around us. Back and forth we reflected each other like a mirror until I smiled and confirmed the lesson had been understood.

We arrived back into the space I recognized: my body inside Alfred's home. She continued to make her potion—opening up jars, getting herbs and spices and mixing them up in her bowl. I could see that making potions brought her great joy as she tapped into that power from within. I ached for that power, for that knowledge of support and connection.

"Once you understand the energetic frequency of the universe, you will see it in everything around you. And you can mold those energies to your desired creations.

You can heal, you can harness, you can create manifestations and live your life to the fullest. All it takes is practice to dance between the worlds, to dance between the seen and the unseen." Alfred said as she poured what was remaining of the powder into her bowl and began mixing. "All it takes is the courage to believe in your ability, in your gifts, and your worth."

"Will you show me how?"

The ceiling above us disappeared, revealing a vast galaxy of twinkling stars. She smiled and winked at me as she pointed above with one hand and rested the other hand on her heart. "There's no wisdom that you don't already know, it's already within you. Wisdom is a form of energy, and like all energy, it can never die. It's simply transformed, waiting for you to call upon it to be revealed." The ceiling closed back up, and Alfred returned to mixing her potions. "But the confidence to act upon the wisdom of the soul is where many suffer. And that is what died with me—the liberation to be who you are without fear. The ability to live as your true self."

I asked Alfred if there was anything else to be revealed, but no new words or ideas came forward. It was merely a reminiscence of what had happened. I was drawn to be shown the themes of the journey once more; the pressure of society for Alfred to hide her powers, and the repercussions of the war that had erupted through the village. And most importantly, the spiritual messages of eternal energy within the vision. I still had many lingering questions, wondering what happened and how. But I felt as though the energy of the journey had played itself out. I was ready to go back into my world and write what I had learned. I knew from my previous journeys that sometimes more messages could come through when I reflected on them. So, I thanked Alfred for her time and I exited her world.

Alfred Reflections

To exit my journey, I took more control of the vision, making sure that my energy had settled in my world as my true self. It's important to do this, because as you are connecting and moving through different energies, you need to ensure that your energy has returned completely and none is left behind.

To do this, I envisioned a miniature version of myself (or sometimes a sphere of light energy—something to represent your soul), and I imagined it entering my body. Often, I will see the stairs from the upper world and walk down into my heart; then the version of myself jumps back inside me, as though it is re-entering its temple, my body.

Sometimes, in journeys, we may find ourselves connecting with spirits we had deep meaningful connections with in past lives. Perhaps an old lover, or friend, that we haven't met in our waking life, so our soul wants to stay with them there. Even though you return to your body, a part of your energy could stay with that spirit, wanting to enjoy that other energy for longer. So, I like to call my energy back into my body. This is a spiritual practice that also works in our waking life whenever we feel our energy is exhausted or drained.

With my eyes closed, I said: "I call all of my energy back into myself. Any energy that I gave away, that was taken or shared, I call it back. And likewise, I give back any energy I have taken." I imagined any elements of light energy that belonged to me, racing along the cosmos and entering my auric field. When I feel like someone else's energy has attached itself to me, I release it from my body through my breath.

Remember, journeying is a process of your soul journeying. It is the energy of your soul moving elsewhere. Your physical body is still here on Earth; it has not moved. As your soul is traveling, your unconsciousness is moving, and you are bringing light to that unconsciousness, hoping to make sense of what you cannot see.

When I finally felt like myself again, I sat up and wrote down everything that had happened: the way that I felt, the visions, the voices, the words, the meanings. Then I just sat still and let my spirit guide me to correlate it all together.

I reflected on the spiritual lessons that Alfred had shared. The repetitive nature of creating potions and harnessing the magic from the land felt like a message in itself for me to heed. My soul is craving to remember the knowledge of how to create such potent concoctions. And this prompted a desire within me to explore some local herbal courses that I could partake in so I could gain that wisdom meticulously. I researched the herbs that she used to create the paste for the injured man. I was amazed to learn that their healing properties were all-natural pain relievers. These were only some of their properties, they each had many more that were scientifically proven.

Rosemary: Anti-inflammatory, high in antioxidants, improves blood circulation and cognitive function.
Black Pepper: Anti-inflammatory, high in antioxidants, supports skin health, and digestion, and boosts immunity.
Turmeric: Anti-inflammatory, high in antioxidants, supports heart health, heals wounds, stomach and digestive disorders, and mood stabilizer.
Aloe Vera: Anti-inflammatory, high in antioxidants, anti-fungal, antiviral, heals wounds, and supports skin health.

I also looked up the name Alfred, and what its meaning was. Alfred means 'magical counsel,' or 'wise elf.' It was perfectly fitting for the kind of person that she was.

The image of floating with Alfred, up in the cosmos, lingered in my mind. And I reflected on the importance of everything having a spirit, having a soul. I knew this was one of the core beliefs from the Indigenous tribes

REMEMBER THE WITCH WITHIN

around the world. And that many of their spiritual practices involved calling out to those spirits for guidance and healing. They were the first people who understood the power of the medicines in the plants. The spirit of that plant would tell them their healing gift. That understanding, of applying the spirit plant's gift to heal the spirit of humans, is one of the most ancient traditional beliefs. The knowledge that we are already aware of, but that is considered 'alternative medicine,' when really, it is natural medicine, it is ancient medicine. It is a medicine that has been practiced for thousands and thousands of years. And conventional medicine, is actually the unusual, modern experiments that we are testing out. It is so new, we don't even know the true repercussions of many products on the market today. Still, despite, the ancient knowledge from plants, many choose to ignore the power of healing from these ancient worlds. And that's okay, I respect that. We should all be allowed to make our own choices for our bodies.

I then reflected on the energy that the journey exuded. The fear I felt from Alfred's life seemed so real to me. I was scared of who was going to knock on the door; I was worried for Alfred's and her daughter's safety. Yet, there was something deeper here at play and I wanted to know more.

Why was this life important for me to view?

Alfred lived in a time when witchcraft and sorcery were punishable by death. She was the last of my bloodline to be able to use her power freely and confidently. And she was the last of my ancestors to be praised for her gifts.

I started to examine how many lives there had been between her life and mine. And I thought about all of the gifts that had been suppressed during that time, and what that meant for me. Their fear of punishment lived in me. It prompted me to question whether this was the real reason I couldn't own my witchcraft heritage.

Is this why I cannot call myself a witch?

I thought of all of the women who came after Alfred, who never had the chance to connect with the spirit world. They didn't have any opportunities to explore their own connection to their soul because it was forbidden. And to live a life without exploring your own belief system, without the presence of love from the other side, seems devastating to me. My spirituality and love for the magical realm gives me life. The voice of spirit has always been interwoven into my entire existence; I feel so closely connected to witchcraft and Gaia so it saddens me that so much of history has been lost. Not only were religions other than Christianity and Islam forbidden in the Middle Ages, but any tools, art, music, poetry, magic, rituals, and spells that represented alternative ideas were destroyed. There was no way to pass on the wisdom that had accumulated except by word of mouth. For this reason alone, witchcraft has been a secret society for hundreds of years.

From the early Middle Ages and onward, a person who disagreed with the systematic structures and organization of the world could be accused of witchcraft. And it wasn't solely the women, but the men too. It was wizards, healers, shamans, artists, poets, philosophers, and many more. Anyone who spoke out against the sovereign was targeted. The government, the monarchy, the churches, were all together on the direct pathway to becoming the great almighty and they were drunk on power. Their actions and laws intentionally created a great division between the peasants and the elites. That gap of inequality and power continued to grow throughout the world and for centuries to come. We may think this was just a time in the past, and that liberty has been gifted, yet we are still living in the repercussions of those early choices.

This pyramid of power that began hundreds of years ago is still alive today, only now, because so much time has passed, the gap between the leaders and the people has become even greater. Therefore, the attempt to overthrow their power seems impossible. The power held by the pyramid is imaginary but it is supported by our collective willingness to comply. We live in a time of strict censorship, where opposing voices, questioning of authority, and the expressions of different opinions are being silenced, and punished. We think we have evolved since the Middle Ages, since the burning of the witches; yet, we are, in fact, faced with the same dilemma—a question of choosing whether to abide by their commands and survive or to walk our truth. We are still those witches who are being burned. Only now, the "burning" is not death, the "burning" is being cast out of society. The burning is the restriction of freedoms. But there is power in numbers, and I believe the pathway to uniting and standing against them begins with harnessing our inner power. We have strength in numbers, when we remember our truth. When we remember the past and what our ancestors went through. And if we examine how we got to this place of discrimination in our lives today, maybe then more of us would wake up, and maybe then more of us would be aware of the truth of what is going on around us and within us.

The stories of those who came before us have been stolen and destroyed. Like Alfred said, we don't know the truth about what really happened. This trauma of stolen land, stolen people, and stolen culture still terrorizes many countries today. Witchcraft and believing in magic was a form of culture. It was a way for people to connect with their souls and understand their life. But that was taken from them. Even now as we try to remember and reveal the pathway that they walked, we cannot because so much of that history has been rewritten—with a biased opinion to suit a particular narrative. We will never really know the truth of what happened, and how they were punished.

Rather than being angry, all I can do is learn from this, heal from this, and make sure others know about it too. Our education and actions are the tools we can use to create peace in the world. Despite the hidden history, I look at our current life, and I am optimistic. This will be the turning point, a time when the people will realize the truth. The consciousness of the world is rising, many chaotic turns of events have forced the world to change, and people want different choices. We are working together to unite this change. But healing our history comes in many forms, we can't just forget and start afresh with one solution that benefits all. The roots of our past are buried deep within the social system of today, and those roots of a small elite group are deeper and more powerful than all the others. They are the few that have control, they are the few that feed the smaller roots. They are the few that will not easily give up their power. Our social system requires entering the most darkest of depths to find the light within and, allow it to illuminate the pathway for equality to take charge. Although this feels grim, we need to remember that all is not lost, for there is power in numbers and there are many slowly waking up to see the truth, the real truth. Not just the truth that we were spoon-fed. We are waking up to reclaim our power.

Selina

Selina

I waited quite some time before journeying again. The reflections on what I had faced during my experience with Alfred continued to resonate within me for several days afterward. I found myself constantly comparing the conflicts she faced to those in my waking world. They correlated so drastically; that it would be easy for me to believe we are doomed. But that's not how I was raised. For I know I'm connected to the entire conscious collective, and that our love will overrule any form of pain, hurt, or misery. We just need to believe in love. I spent the next few days continuing to write and reflect, trying my best to relay my own emotional journey alongside the vision. My experiences translated deeper than what words can form; they are a feeling. When the time finally came to journey again, I eagerly ignited my ritual, wondering which past life was going to show itself to me next, and in what way. Most importantly, how will this help others?

As I ascended the staircase, I saw the king and queen sitting in the same position as before—right in the center of the upper world. This time, I noticed their surroundings in more detail. They sat upon pale green wooden chairs with very straight backs. The wood was incised with an intricate floral design, with small petals and leaves poking out from the main structure. Their majesties were dressed as before, in blue robes, complete with crowns. Behind them was a blurred, light blue backdrop with no beginning, and no end, it just was.

The queen stood up and placed one hand on my heart and the other on my forehead. "The pathway before you now will awaken an unusual feeling inside, but be brave and do not be scared, for it is merely energy."

I nodded in response, signaling that I understood. The king stayed seated but watched our interaction with a faint smile. Then the queen walked me to the left path, the path of my past life. As I walked toward it, it turned into a slide. I waved goodbye and thanked them as I slid down it, twirling around until I arrived at a small pond.

I frolicked in the water for a while, allowing my body to soak up all its goodness. The sensations felt liberating. There was a feeling of deep peace in the pond, a combination of the perfect temperature and nutritious minerals on my skin. I felt as though I was swimming in my mother's womb, deeply held and nurtured. When I felt ready to exit, I was pulled in one direction. I surrendered to the current and soon reached a small beach. There was sand all around me and a large forest of beautiful tall trees. It was nighttime. My energy gravitated toward the trees to my right and, as I walked through them, I spied a large bonfire. A group of naked women and men were dancing all around.

The people were moving fast, swirling their arms up high and swaying their bodies back and forth. They appeared translucent-like, almost as though what I was seeing was the color of their energetic aura dancing around them. Together they flowed in a fluent circle around the large fire, prancing and twirling up high and low. I noticed one woman standing close to the fire, but separate from the circle of dancers. She had pale, almost silver, skin and long silver hair with a green-leafed crown around it. She wore a long silver gown. She was staring intently into the flames, her palms open toward them, feeling the heat. What's your name? I asked in my mind. "Selina" I heard the voice say back.

I stood next to her, but the energy between us was so strong, it pulled me right into her. Within seconds, I found myself merging with her energy. I kept trying to pull myself back, to watch from afar, but it was impossible. For I was witnessing a past life where she was me, I was her. At this stage of my journey, the energy within me felt intense and heavy. I felt as though I had just multiplied exponentially for I was taking on her energy in addition to my own. At last, I remembered what the queen had said before I had entered this life. I released the need to control and trusted that I would be shown what was needed. I surrendered to the vision and allowed myself to become Selina.

We looked at the fire together, and as we did, she told me we were becoming the fire. We walked closer to the flames and I felt a surplus of heat cocoon my body. And when we walked deeper into the fire, we shriveled up quickly, transforming before my very eyes.

"Fire transforms all matter into another frequency. The naked eye sees matter turn to smoke and ash, and we too mirror that transformation, but there is a transformation of the emotional and spiritual energy as well. You just can't see it, but you can feel it." I heard the voice come from within me. Was it my voice or hers? I wasn't sure. Although if I had been her at some point, her words were mine.

I felt myself float up high above the fire; higher, and higher, past the trees, past the planet, and up into the galaxy. I felt euphoric, a feeling I had never had before, and one my rational mind wanted to understand. "Perhaps I'm dreaming," my mind said. But Selina quickly corrected me, and I found myself saying, "I am seeing and feeling the truth."

After floating in space, Selina took me to what appeared to be another planet, for we had traveled far from where we had started. The imagery of what lay before us, made me question—which was Earth? The land where we now stood upon was a field of high yellow grass; a vision that very well could have been from my waking life. I held my hand out, allowing the grass to tickle my skin as I looked up high into the sky. It displayed a glorious bouquet of pastel hues, yellow, orange, and pink colors, as the sun was setting in the distance. It was beautiful. The imagery and colors resembled those of Earth, as did the previous scene in the forest by the fire, and it confused me. Were we just on Earth, dancing around the fire with others? Or was this Earth now?

The question of multiple dimensions circulated in my mind, as a vision of simultaneous lives played out before me. I saw myself expand and retract across each lifeline, as though holographic images of myself took control. I was living in a multiverse. Each of those versions had its own life, and was living its own reality. The spiral continued to spin. My vision focused on one of the cut-out figures, and it magnified within it, revealing an entirely new spiral inside it. It was a fractal, one spiral continuing after the other, each spiral containing an entire world of its own. Each world that replayed before me showed me a magnitude of sacred geometry. As my gaze zoomed in on one of the lives, I could see each element holding its own fractal spiral inside it. The trees, leaves, and petals, were all expanding with definition and colors. Each object continued to expand with intricate patterns. I was mesmerized by the beauty. The fluidity of the motion trapped itself within me, and I hallucinated with this vision for only a few moments, but those seconds felt like hours.

But then something very strange happened. The energy of traveling so fast and so far made me feel dizzy. It was as though my whole body had been spinning turbulently, out of control. Nausea rushed up through my stomach and into my head. The energy was circulating too quickly, and my mind was trying desperately to catch up. But it was failing. I had no other option but to wake myself up from this journey hurriedly.

I opened my eyes and cradled myself back in my body. Still, the energy was circulating chaotically within me. I needed to use my breath to calm myself, to bring peace back into my heart once more. After several minutes of slow deep breathing, I reclaimed my ease. When I had gathered my presence, I reflected on Selina and my experience with her. I held a great desire to embody the wisdom that I had witnessed; I wanted to step into that fearless version of myself. But the energy had swirled too dramatically, and I had cowered away. Then I reminded myself of my power as I saw the vision of Selina in my mind. I repeated the words in my head, "I am one with the Universe. I am one with the Universe." And I felt my inner strength grow with confidence. I always say this mantra whenever I feel uneasy. If I feel that something is beyond my control, I remind myself that, although I cannot influence the outcome, I can control my reaction. So I choose to allow the energy to flow through me. I enable my body to be an alchemist and to transmute those feelings.

When I was sure that my energy had settled, I braced myself for a return journey. I needed to see what else was to be learned from Selina. In all of my years of journeying to the outer realms, it was my first experience of visiting an alternative reality. Although the thoughts of alternate universes had crossed my mind before, I had not expected such a feeling of grounding, as I had experienced on Earth. Instead of feeling that I didn't belong anywhere, I felt that, in fact, I belonged in both places and that this was my soul's decision to come here and experience my life. There was a flicker of hope within me, an understanding of the energy around me and I wanted to know more. So, without much consideration, I held the vision of Selina clear in my head, and I ignited my ritual once again.

Selina II

I closed my eyes and entered a meditative trance. Calling out to the universal energies, I allowed their presence to lead the pathway. But when I left my body, I did not return to the upper world, and to the kingdom of the gatekeepers. Instead, I saw a circle on the ground open up; a slide protruded and beckoned my energy downward. I took a step onto the slide, and it whooshed me down quickly. Down, down, down. Until I arrived at what appeared to be a small cave. The walls were covered in mud, in a rich orange color. On my right was an enormous wall of flames. Strangely, it reminded me of an image that I had described in one of my fantasy books from the Lost Nowhere series, where the main character, Lily, arrives in the center of her magical world, a space full of molten lava. I've had this happen before, where I have visited past lives, or had visions during meditations, of places I had created in my books. And the question still remains: Which came first? My imagination? Or was my imagination remembering these places from my own past experiences? The more often I journey, the more I come to believe it is the latter.

I was confused as to why I was standing there, amidst the volcanic lava, until Selina appeared before me in a flash. "I'm sorry I left hurriedly," I began to explain, but there was no need. Selina took my hand and we began floating back in the galaxy again. I felt weightless, with an immense sensation of peace surrounding me. It was as though we were souls drifting through the galaxy, immersed in source energy, waiting to enter our next life.

Selina took me back down to the ground to show me her life—our life. And I watched as though it was a movie playing out before me, yet it felt familiar. "This is my home," she said, as she showed me a cozy wooden cabin in the middle of a forest. My vision changed to a birds-eye view, seeing Selina's house as the sole structure in a gigantic forest. The trees were over 100 feet tall, with large bushy branches all clustered together. The ground was covered in snow. Selina needed to wear thick high boots to walk around. There was a small chimney with a gentle stream of smoke coming out of it. It was an idyllic place, one I would have loved to visit for a holiday; but to live there, I would have felt so secluded, isolated from others.

"I never bore children." Selina continued. "I never shared my life with another." There was no sadness in her statement. No feeling of having missed out. It was just a different path.

When I asked Selina where she was from, what planet she lived on, or what the year was. There was no answer. The year 11211 came through to me at one point, but this was so far into the future that I could never think it possible to experience it. Or, were we on another planet entirely?

I saw an image of Selina transform from a ragged woman into the silver goddess-like figure I had met by the fire. Which one was she? The answers within me said she was both. Many of the village folk perceived her as a crazy lady living in the forest; yet to the people who lived as she did, she was a high priestess, a divinity of angelic energy. I wanted to know more about her teaching, about her way of life, and about what she did in this world. And, what was this world?

"Come with me," she said, reading my thoughts. She took me into the forest.

She walked up to a tree and placed her hand on its trunk, simulating a spark of lightning to ignite. The lightning transformed into a ball of yellow energy and it flickered with soft pulsations, signaling that it was alive and vibrant. Selina closed her eyes lovingly and my vision followed the light energy that had erupted from her hand as it moved into her heart, then traveled down through the tree. The light moved along the tree trunk, then separated as it reached the ground, wriggling through all the roots deep into the dirt.

When the vibrating light connected with the other trees' roots, it set them ablaze, like a fire, exploding light energy into fine lines. I witnessed an illuminated web of blazing light strings, weaving through the entire planet and circulating around and around in one never-ending spinning sphere. It signified the truthful connection of wholeness and unity.

 Another ball of light ignited from Selina's hand, and it followed the same destiny, moving over to her heart, and then bouncing back down through the tree and into the earth. It sparkled fiercely as it separated through the roots and then joined the cosmic web too. Then Selina created another light ball and another and another. Each light ball gained more and more momentum as it moved along the tree, through the roots, and into the earth, one after the other. She continued to create the balls of light until all of the illuminated energy moved so quickly that it appeared as one continuous stream of light vibrating from her body and into the ground. The light cords were electrifying, vibrating loudly with brilliant color. They lit up the entire planet with a beautiful pattern, through the trees, through their roots, and into the dirt. Selina was giving her energy to the trees, and they too were feeding theirs back to her. It was a constant flow of giving and receiving and she was igniting it through just her intention and touch.

Selina took a step back and encouraged me to repeat her actions. I held my hand out and touched the tree, mirroring her connection. A light ignited from my body, but it was much fainter than hers, and I felt disappointed.

"It will take practice," Selina reassured me.

I tried again and again until I mimicked her exact motion and, finally, I achieved the success of illuminating the space as she had done. As I played my role, I felt a deep sense of peace grounding and soothing in my soul. As though I had come home to a space where I belonged. A space that I had been craving. I had no idea I had desired such a feeling until now. Although the energy was vibrating quickly, I felt at ease, I felt at peace. It flowed as though it was merely an extension of my own energy field.

I thought I had mastered the lessons of nature. I knew that the energy of the tree and Mother Earth had the ability to bring forth new sensations. But it's what came next that made me see the universe and its creation differently.

"What is the purpose of this connection?" I asked.

Selina turned to face me and held my hands tightly. Her touch was electrifying, a moment of blissful exhilaration and I felt my body shiver with pleasure.

"We, as souls, travel to different worlds to connect with the energy of the planets. From here, we are able to feed our soul with heightened vibrations. These vibrations have the ability to contribute to the growth of our soul. We can go to any planet, any world we desire. But why? So often we think we are there to live as a human and to reconnect the connection between our soul and body. But really, our purpose in life is to connect with the energy of the planet. And to allow our energy to be transformed by all of the sensations around us. Fill yourself up with the vibrations of earth, air, water, fire, and other spirits. Here is where we …"

Her voice drifted off, yet I felt completely transformed from within, as though a light had pierced through my perception of the world, changing it forever. I already knew how important it was to connect with the vibrations of Mother Nature, of Earth and the sensations of those around me. But for those connections to be our sole purpose? For that interaction to be our chief of importance? I had never thought of that before.

Selina carried me up high into the sky, and together we drifted until we arrived at the world we had visited before. Although, it was now evident that this was another planet entirely. The sky had turned into a dark pink hue and a soft breeze rustled through the tall yellow grass.

"Feel this energy," Selina whispered, although I could not see her anymore. "Feel the energy this world brings you."

The emotions I felt in this moment were so obscure to me that I couldn't even find the words to describe them. There was a sense of tranquility different from anything I had ever felt before. On Earth we feel grounded when immersed in nature—balanced and harmonized. But here, there was the feeling of lightness. I felt as though I appeared translucent, and that there was no separation between me and the world around me. I was completely connected to the horizon, completely connected to the grass, like I was in all places at once.

I enjoyed this energy for several minutes, trying to comprehend the surfacing emotions. Every time I tried, the feelings settled deeper into my subconscious, becoming one with me, and escaping definition. I had nothing to compare them to. In other words, it wasn't something I was feeling for a moment, it was in me, the energy became me, and this was my new feeling. But that feeling was peace. That feeling was blissful energy, and lightness of being. I felt like I was coming home to myself.

No new images came through to me after this. I asked to exit the journey. I felt myself float back to the top of the staircase of the upper world. I think perhaps I was carried down by Selina, for the process was so gradual, so gentle, I felt like I was held like a sleeping baby, carefully so as not to be awoken. I returned to the golden staircase, with water flowing gently over the sides. From there I walked back down into my waking reality, and into my body.

Selina Reflections

When I emerged from my journey, I felt as though a great epiphany had washed over me. And I lay there for several minutes trying to absorb the information and incorporate it into my understanding. I felt as though I'd had a severe alteration of my world perspective from Selina's potent lessons.

Was our life here on Earth purely to feel different energies? Is that what truly influenced the transformation of our soul? Or were our life lessons crucial to our evolution?

I could understand Selina's theory from a scientific standpoint, for everything is energy. Our relationships, our experiences, our ability to love another—it's all energy that influences the transformation of our soul. But the actual process of transformation, I believe comes from within. At the core of my belief system is that our reality is a manifestation of our own internal perception. In other words, the way we perceive the outside world is a direct reflection of the energy we hold in our inner world. We make the world around us because of how we see it. How we see it is a direct reflection of how we feel from the energy we radiate. During this journey with Selina, she told me that our soul's energy transforms because of outside energy

REMEMBER THE WITCH WITHIN

forces, not just the way we perceive the energy. She explained that it's not solely our internal energy, but also the energy we receive from the natural resources around us. And when we come into contact with that energy around us, it's up to us to be the alchemist that transmutes that energy to feed our soul. And that in turn, transforms our energy field. There were certainly elements of truth in Selina's belief. Either way we look at our life, we are always connecting with energy, whether it be that of another being or the planet. Our life lessons just give us the motive to move in the direction we need to go. And maybe, because of the hardships that we face in our life, we are forced to turn to the Earth to heal ourselves through its energy. Thereby, supporting Selina's concept of our soul's purpose to feed ourselves with these vibrations.

Although as I explain this, I feel like I already knew this, and you may too. As Alfred said, wisdom is created and all we are doing is tapping into that wisdom, that we already knew once upon a time. But, there's something deeper here to be revealed. So I sat with my experience with Selina for some time trying to grasp her message and make sense of it. We receive energy and that, in turn, affects our energy. The energy we emit also affects the energy around us. If the catch and release, giving and receiving, of energy is a constant flow, how do we know which is our own energy? Or is it all our energy? There was only one way to find out; I needed to apply this idea to my current reality.

My waking life didn't reflect the depth of emotional attachment I felt to the energy I received during my journey with Selina. I immersed myself in nature, walking through the forest like we had done by her cabin in the woods. But there was something missing. As I moved closer to a tree to feel its energy as I'd be shown, my mind restricted me from moving forward. I felt my ego taking over, telling me that I looked silly and that I needed to be careful in case someone saw me doing this. I argued with my mind, insisting that I was in charge. Even as I write this, it sounds crazy, but it's true. I needed to tell my mind: Enough!

When I began breathing deeply, the voice in my head melted away; there is no space for mind chatter when I am meditating. When I meditate, I create an unbreakable bond with the universe, with my soul in the unseen realms, and this provides me with guidance and wisdom. When I meditate, I ground myself, and establish that connection; all I hear is the voice of self-love coming from my heart. I let that loving voice speak louder; I ask for its support in achieving this moment of connection. And I ignore anything else around me.

As I touched the tree and my mind became quiet, the sound of nature sang ever so sweetly, calming my energy to resonate with its soothing beat. I released any expectations and I surrendered to the present moment. Allowing my breath to become still, I opened myself to receive the energy of the tree before me. I used my intention, asking to feel its love. I told it that I wanted to give it my energy too. I imagined the blaze of light I had created with Selina, and slowly, very slowly, my energy began to change. I felt an inkling of heat ignite between my hand and the bark of the tree. I continued to breathe slowly and, as I imagined the flame of light moving from me into the tree, I could feel the heat amplify.

Creating energy between your hands with your intention is one of the first practices in energy healing. I was doing exactly that, except that instead of using my two hands, it was one hand and the surface of the tree. We were creating energy between us because we were both alive. The tree was sending its energy to me and I was sending mine to the tree. I felt an overwhelming sensation of pure joy in my heart. A blissful high that erupted throughout my whole body. It reminded me of the feeling I had when I swam in the pond on my journey to see Selina. Only now, the womb no longer felt of my mother, it was clearly that of Mother Nature, and I was being nurtured and healed with her love.

But the questions remained unanswered. *Is the energy I am receiving also the energy I am creating? Where do I begin and end? Is the tree an extension of my own creation?* Instead of dwelling on these questions, I simply embraced the moment. I allowed myself to be filled up with the energy of Mother Nature. I embodied her beauty within me and opened myself up to receive her healing love.

I do not fear that my questions will be left unanswered; rather, the answers will be presented to me at the right and perfect time. Until then....

Bonita

Bonita

The next day, I felt an overwhelming sense of excitement to journey again. Visiting these lives gave me a great sense of connection with the spiritual realm, and I enjoyed it immensely. It was a safe space to play in, and I was able to discover profound wisdom while doing so. As soon as I could, I opened up my ritual space to meet the next life. But as I connected with the universal energies and called upon their blessings, I felt different. I felt more connected to them this time, and I could feel the changes they created within me. Or rather, I could feel how I changed my own energetic vibration from their presence.

When I began beating my drum to ignite my trance, I could feel the vibration resonate deeply within me. I opened myself to truly embody that sound, allowing myself to fall deeper and deeper into relaxation. The golden staircase soon appeared before me; I ascended, as before, to be met by the king and queen. They were waiting for me, seated and dressed like before. But this time they said no words. There was just peace in presence. I knew that if I asked anything, they would answer, but there was nothing to be shared. They were merely the gatekeepers, wise counselors who protected and served the spirit realm.

I walked toward the paths, sensing which one would captivate me today. I immediately felt myself pulled toward the right path, to the past lives of my ancestors. The pathway turned into a long slanted hill, and I slid down it quickly. To my surprise, when I landed, I had arrived once more at Alfred's wooden door. I felt a bit of resistance to move forward. An inkling of doubt moved through my mind. I wondered if I was imagining the whole experience. Why had I arrived in Alfred's world again? I scolded myself for having become too confident in my journeys, and too eager in my excitement. And like all negative thoughts, my mood spiraled quickly. But instead of feeding that negativity, I spoke to my soul, asking for guidance. It told me there was more to be revealed in this life.

When I looked at the door, it flung open and I was pulled into the kitchen. I was standing in front of Alfred. She held a large clay bowl in one hand and a wooden mixing spoon in the other; she was mixing the potions as usual. She smiled as though signaling a knowing that I would return.

But instead of talking with Alfred, I was pulled toward Bonita's energy shining in the corner. I realized my journey to Alfred's was not actually about her, but rather, about the life of her daughter, and what was to become of it.

REMEMBER THE WITCH WITHIN

But Bonita wouldn't look at me. She was staring straight ahead. I felt as though there was a lack of connection between the mother and daughter. Bonita was now a teenager, and she held great shame. She sat in the corner with rough ragged clothing, and dirt in her hair.

"What good is understanding the magic of the universe if I am hungry?" Bonita asked me, continuing to stare at the wall, not acknowledging my presence.

I felt a heavy weight in my heart as I looked at her. I empathized with her frustration. Her question summarized how I felt about my life's work at the beginning of my career: writing, connecting with the spirit realm, and channeling messages, yet unable to make enough money to eat. But comprehending the universe and its magical ways supported a different realm of fulfillment in me. Because through it I was able to develop many spiritual tools that enabled me to have a stronger connection with my soul. This was the most important life lesson I could ever master. Because of this, I was able to create my life-long passion into my career. I began to hear the voice of my soul more clearly, accepting its guidance. Learning how to listen to my intuition was one of the most important spiritual practices I ever mastered, for it enabled me to overcome any difficulties in my life.

But Bonita didn't have the opportunities to support delving deep within herself. She had no time to learn who she was or how she could develop a connection with her soul because she was too hungry. The Middle Ages was a period of long working hours with very little rewards. The women worked all day making money and then fulfilled their household duties of cooking, cleaning, and taking care of the children. The women never rested and were barely praised. Bonita needed to abide by the laws and conform. She was just trying to survive, yet I could feel her desire to become someone greater than the limitations imposed upon her.

When I asked for Bonita to show me her life, she responded so quickly. It was as though she had been waiting for me too. Within seconds, she stood up, opened the front door, and rushed me outside.

Together we walked along a dirt pathway through the village and under a bridge until we arrived at a small house. There was a man standing in front of the side door, and he motioned for us to come inside. I looked to Bonita, awaiting her approval.

"It's alright," she said and nodded, encouraging me to walk through the door. "We're allowed to do this. It's all that's allowed to be practiced now. Everything else is illegal. Everything else is punishable by death."

It appeared as a tiny stone cottage from the outside, but when I entered it was filled with many rows of people sitting in prayer. At the front of the room was a crucifix. I now understood that Bonita was not just ashamed of Alfred being a healer, it was also the religious beliefs of the community that hindered her life experience.

Bonita took a seat on the aisle and bowed her head; she began reciting bible verses but coyly looked at the man sitting opposite her. He returned her gaze with intensity, completely immersed in her presence.

"That man, look at his clothes. We've never seen such wealth before." Bonita whispered, continuing to hold her gaze.

At this moment, I realized Bonita had not only disowned her mother's gifts, but she had chosen the opposition, the religion of the monarchy. It was a choice that supported the patriarchy, and therefore influenced the entire conscious collective, changing the direction of power for centuries to come. Whether Bonita believed in religion was not important, for if Bonita was to align with the god before her, it could be her exit from poverty. She would no longer need to hide with her mother and rather, open an invitation to meet others who could raise her social status.

An elderly gentleman entered the front of the room and everyone stopped their prayers. He appeared to be the priest, in his long black robe. There was something different about him.

"He has traveled from the city. We don't get folks like him much 'round here." Bonita said, looking at me quickly, and then back to the young man she was flirting with.

The priest raised his hands as he began to talk to the crowd. I had difficulty understanding what he was saying, but I could feel his energy. His message held strength and comfort. He had smiling eyes, and there was safety behind them. He was a charismatic kind of fatherly figure and I had a craving to get to know him.

"They're talking about people like my mother," Bonita said. "He's telling the village people to be careful of those who don't come to church. He's calling them pagans. He says they are traitors of God. He says that they can't be trusted."

The village folk all looked around at each other, taking note of who was there and who wasn't. The division had already begun, and the elderly man with the perceived power was enforcing it.

My journey began to slow down at that point. As the people re-enacted the same gestures of prayer and peering at each other, over and over again. I wondered if perhaps this was my soul or my spirit guide's way of telling me to take note, that this was an important piece of information. Or, maybe there was nothing more to be learned here. I set my intention once more. *What else is there to be learned of Bonita's life?*

My vision then flashed ahead to Bonita and the young man she had been flirting with. They were getting married. They stood there, before the priest, taking the vows. Finally, I thought, Bonita was going to get the life that she craved.

After the wedding, Bonita showed me where they lived and what had become of her life. Together we traveled far, over mountains and across many rivers. When we finally arrived I saw that she had now married into middle-class wealth. Bonita did, in fact, achieve her goals in life. She had a decadent house, on top of a hill, just above a small village. She bore six children, four boys and two girls. She had safety and security, and most importantly, warm food for herself and her children. She had received the luxuries she desired, and the life of poverty was a distant memory. But there was one problem. Something was missing from her life. Something that couldn't be bought. But she didn't realize it until she grew old, and her children grew older and all left her alone in the house with her husband. It was then she realized that she didn't belong there.

She walked around the rooms, which were filled with expensive paintings, yet she felt so empty. For she realized, that she didn't truly own any of it. Not just *own*, she didn't *choose* any of it. It just existed before her. This wasn't her house, this wasn't her life. She was living her husband's life, she was living in *his* house, and she realized that her presence in this world had been solely to support him. She hadn't been aware of any of this because she had been busy. She had been busy getting herself out of poverty and achieving her lavish dreams. She had been busy creating beautiful children and raising them with love. She had been busy, ignoring the voice of her soul, ignoring the very lessons her mother used to teach her. She had been too busy to visit Alfred. And, by the time she visited her mother, it was too late. Alfred had already passed over. Alfred had already left the seen realms and had taken all of her wisdom with her.

Bonita II

The vision of Bonita's life gave me great sadness. After Alfred died, Bonita barely left her bedroom. And she sat there alone, looking out to the grand city before her, yet feeling untouchable and disconnected. She never found a friend who liked her for who she was. She only had acquaintances, those who were attracted to her wealth above her personality. She had chased this wealth all her life and gave up her soul in the process of doing so. Bonita felt as though there was something missing in her life. She was always searching. But she never found what she was looking for.

"I played the part they wanted me to," Bonita told me as she lay in her bed, close to death. "I followed the path of the Lord, I married and bore children. I was loyal and respectful to my husband. That was all I was allowed. I thought I was benefiting from this situation. I lived a life of comfort and didn't have to do much. But that was the problem. When I finally realized I wanted to do more, I wasn't allowed. The rules were so subtle; I didn't know what I was giving up until it was too late."

The journey ended with me seeing Bonita on her deathbed. She told me, she held regret. She told me that she wished she could have made different choices.

But, having been faced with starvation, being an outcast, and feeling shame for being who she was, she felt she didn't really have a choice. She needed to fit in to survive, she needed to give up her truth for the sake of her children. The price she paid gave her comfort, yet what came with it was boredom and no freedom.

When I returned to my body I wanted to research the lifestyles from that era to understand the pressures Bonita had been under to make the choices she did.

The early Middle Ages was a time when agriculture accelerated dramatically. This generated wars for valuable resources, such as fertile land. The people worked in the fields for long hours with little remuneration. However, some were able to make enough money to acquire their own land, which they needed to protect. Land could only be owned by the man and only the sons could inherit that land, unless the female was an only child. But even then, once she married, the husband would take ownership of that inheritance. The women worked long hours making money for their families, caring for their children, and fulfilling their household duties, while obeying their husbands. And in return, the women were given nothing. They couldn't make decisions of importance, they couldn't own anything. They were the property of their husband. And so, the hierarchy of power began, with the men at the top and the women down far below.

Seeing this separation explained the importance of my arrival in Bonita's life when I did. For it was where and when the great change took place in many aspects of daily life. The shift in power between men and women amplified. The value of money and political power intensified. The change of religion and control of the people escalated. This was when the suppression of women took charge, when freedom of speech and the liberty to follow one's beliefs was punished. Those changes caused chaos in the world for centuries to come. Except now, this dangerous vision has grown thick roots deep within the Earth, taking hold of the collective unconsciousness. We are obeying to its rules without even realizing it.

The Middle Ages was a time when Christianity took control of the Western world, encouraging the destruction of paganism—to be enforced by law and punishable by death. This was a process that took hundreds of years; it was a gradual conversion that took place one person at a time. The church eventually grew to hold the greatest power over the country. They taxed the people to support the faith, which created both wealth and power for the church. In return, the people were promised salvation. The church was growing more powerful than the country's leaders, and so, the empires had no choice but to side with the church, for the power that the church possessed was able to take control of them at any point. If those in power chose to ignore the voice of the church, they would be cast aside themselves. The laws were made with the guidance of priests, bishops, and clergy. Mankind was faced with great wars, plagues, and famine, and only the church was able to provide comfort and solutions in these dire times by promising a safe afterlife by God's side.

The only way for Bonita to find peace was to side with the leaders, to become one with the majority. For if she were to believe in anything other than Christianity, she would have been killed. If she hadn't left her mother's home and sought refuge with another, she would have died from her association with a witch. When Bonita made her choice, she wasn't really thinking it through. She was thinking of a warm bed, of food on her plate, clothes on her back and a man to love her. She was thinking of the necessities of life that so many take for granted. She thought sacrificing her beliefs to provide safety and protection for her offspring was the right choice.

Although I could understand her need for security and survival, I couldn't help but correlate how this choice helped shape the society I live in today. Bonita's decision to ignore her powers, to choose Christianity, changed not only her life but that of our bloodline and the whole of humanity. By abandoning her beliefs, Bonita supported the growth of patriarchy.

In the Middle Ages, only a man could be a priest, only men were allowed in the clergy, and only men were allowed to make important worldly decisions. If a woman wanted to take on responsibility, she would have been ridiculed. And although we can understand that Bonita was just trying to survive, the repercussions of her choice, live on many generations later. Certainly, it was not a choice only Bonita made; she is simply a metaphor for *all* women who gave up their power in exchange for safety and security.

Bonita didn't know that remaining submissive enabled the patriarchy to grow. She didn't know that she played her part in maintaining inequality. She didn't know. But had she known, would she have made a different choice?

I could see her decision and its impact so clearly. It was as though this choice of Bonita's to suppress her true identity had solidified into a brick, and that she had placed that first brick on a wall of resistance. With each life that came after hers, those of her children, her children's children, and their children's children, all placed a brick on that wall to conceal their power. So, by the time I was born, that brick wall had been standing for many moons. That brick wall had been built gradually with strength and articulate intention, so to destroy it would take greater strength, persistence, and much healing. That wall symbolized unhealed ancestral trauma, a massive blockage of generational flow. To dismantle it would be my first mission.

If I were faced with the question of survival versus holding tightly to my beliefs, what would I do? I wondered if I would do the same. Life in the 21st century has, for the most part, evolved beyond mere survival. Now we can access ancient spiritual tools to find deeper meaning in our lives to create our own happiness without being punished. Now we are presented with opportunities to heal and learn from our mistakes, and to make a real difference. We have choices at our fingertips that allow us to harness our own power. We have the time to find our medicine, polish our talents, and share our gifts with the world. But in order to do all of this, we need the confidence to step into our authentic selves without fear. And the only way we can do that is by believing in ourselves and taking action for equality for all.

Because, despite the numerous opportunities we have, there's still inequality. Not all opportunities are equal. Too many people are still cast aside. Too many are punished and suppressed based on race, religious views, sexual preferences, and gender. There are still many people like Bonita who are forced to make choices they don't want in order to survive. We are living in a world where freedom is given to us by the elite, and we are told to believe that we have it, yet it is merely an illusion. For we are being forced to survive amidst the freedom between the walls they have created. We are still so busy, trying to secure the basic necessities of shelter, food, and warmth, that we don't see what they are really doing. And how they are stealing our power.

Our actions and thoughts are influenced by our upbringing. We go through our lives inundated with carefully constructed marketing and advertising. This false narrative relays our survival rules and regulations. And this protocol is packaged and delivered by an elite group who hold the power. An elite group, consisting of white men, that has evolved beyond the clergy, beyond the government; it is a very wealthy minute group of puppeteers that control the people by pulling the strings. Those strings force the patriarchal system to grow, those strings keep the hierarchy alive, and those strings divide the community. We need to cut the strings and think for ourselves. We need to remember where it is that we came from. We need to remember the truth of our own divinity.

The only way through to healing and reclaiming our truth is to recognize, acknowledge, and understand what happened before us, and how that negatively impacts us. We need to reveal and understand why humanity acted the way it did, and discover whether those actions are now outdated. For all of our emotions, our intentions, and our beliefs are the result of our ancestral behavior and our past lives. We are repeating the same mistakes unless we learn from them.

Instead of just being angry about our history and the world around us, I allowed it to feed me, to give me the ammunition needed to change the future. It gave me a sense of peace and hope that I could make that change because I now know how my choices can impact this world.

I felt at peace in knowing that what happened to my ancestors caused a shift in my self-worth. I understood that my lack of confidence surrounding my true self wasn't created only in this life, but had been building for many generations. I hoped I could find the power within to create change, for I knew that power existed in me before. But to make changes that would ripple through future generations would require me to re-examine myself and those around me. My own life would be the beginning point, and then I would journey back and back and back, and continue to heal the resistance of those who came before me. I couldn't change their actions or decisions, but I could strive to empathize with their lives, and understand what forced them to make their choices.

Hidden in the past was a wounded female who chose to fall. Hidden in the past was a powerful goddess who concealed her talents in order to survive. But in this life, we have a choice. We have the gift of opportunity, the first of its kind in hundreds of years. We have an opportunity to remember the power of our truth, of our authenticity. We have found the entry point to recognize how to remember the witch within.

Gabriella

Gabriella

It had been many months since I'd journeyed to visit my past lives and ancestors. Summer had begun and I was completely besotted with the fertile power of the present moment, traveling and enjoying experiences with friends. I had never felt such depth of emotions by living so freely with happiness and love. And I rejoiced in those moments.

But fall soon came and went, and I was left with the darkness of a cold winter once more. This time of year had always been the most challenging for me; I strived to find that determined little girl within me—resilient and confident—so that I could persevere. The lack of sunlight and cold winds weighed heavy on my heart and I often found myself lost and ungrounded. This had happened to me many times before. I knew that the solution to get me out of this mind frame was the diligent repetition of spiritual practices and, most importantly, having a sense of purpose.

With this in mind, I decided to commit to journeying for the next few weeks. I needed to find myself, find my purpose in my life, and to ground myself. Whenever I am ungrounded, it is because my spiritual routine has not been cemented in place. And because I had allowed myself to flow freely through the warm months without a solid routine, it made sense that I had lost it. I needed to mend all the chaos that I had allowed to affect me.

This next journey I am to share was a difficult one to endure. I felt troubled energy circulating and many questions surfacing. I wondered if my mind had taken over, and whether it reflected the hardship of my current waking surroundings. Usually, I turned to my inner world journeys to gain peace and beauty, but this one showed me the opposite. Like all past lives, it is a part of me.

After opening up my ritual space, I was immediately pulled to the upper world. The pull from my soul into this realm was intense. Instead of the usual straight ascending staircase, it was a spiral. And I walked around and around beginning to feel quite dizzy.

When I finally reached the top of the staircase, I did not find my king and queen. Instead, I stood upon a finely-powdered-dirt cliff, with nothing before me, but bleakness and a woman. She had a depth of anguish on her face and her ghostly presence was haunting. But I wasn't scared; I felt sorrow. I was sad that this was what I was drawn to in my current state of despair. I was searching for safety and love, but was, instead, confronted with my own misery.

The woman looked as though she was in her late 40s; she had faint wrinkles on her face, and scruffy brown hair. Her attire reminded me of someone who belonged in a mental asylum, a long cream-colored nightdress with long sleeves. When she saw me, she hunched over into a ball, screaming and crying and holding herself tightly.

I crouched next to her, took her in my arms, and held her lovingly.

"Gabriella," she whispered. She began to tell me her story. Not her whole story, just a crucial part of her story.

Gabriella believed that she was separate from source energy, separated from the cosmic collective. She couldn't escape this isolation she had created. I pitied her and wanted to help. Perhaps I recognized myself in her. My first instinct was to help her heal the same way I heal myself. My own mental health suffers when there is a block of energy within me. I wondered if perhaps Gabriella was reflecting my own misery. If she was, then just like me, she was the one creating her imbalance. I wanted to shake the stuck energy out of her, but it wasn't that simple. For, as I shook her body trying to talk sense into her, I was told that she was indeed one of my past lives, not just a reflection of my current life. But even though I was told this, I couldn't help but correlate the two. For Gabriella was mirroring my exact current emotions.

And, I wanted to help her. I needed to help her, for this would, in turn, help me, and hopefully heal an unconscious aspect of my life. So I helped her, in the same way I had learned how to help myself.

"Let's find your purpose," I said to Gabriella, as I looked to the dirt landscape laid out before us. I took her hand and encouraged her to dig into the ground.

"Let's make a home," I said, knowing the importance of finding a safe space to start. And so we began to build a small muddy hut on top of the dirt.

Once the first hut was finished, I felt a calling to make more. So we did. We built another, and another. Each hut was more elaborate and detailed than the last. Some had windows, and others we painted. We were creating a safe space for Gabriella to heal. We were creating a sacred place for her to call home, where she could feel like she belonged. Satisfied that we had created a moment of distraction for her, a moment out of her painful perception of the world around her. But it was only a moment. As soon as we had finished creating the mud huts, she sat back down on the ground with her head in her hands, and began crying once more.

The mud houses disappeared.

Realizing what was missing in her life, I said, "You need to believe in the higher power around you." I showed her the sky and the universe all around us. "You need to feel the support of the energy that created you. And remember that you, in turn, create the energy that surrounds you."

The sky above turned into nighttime and a galaxy of stars appeared, shining brightly. I gazed at their presence with great awe and admiration.

"You are divinely guided always," I continued. "Believe in yourself, believe in the universe, believe in miracles." I held her hands and looked into her eyes, I was searching for her soul. I called out to it again. "There is beauty within you. There is talent inside of you. You are never alone. You are always connected and supported by the Divine."

I could see a small flicker of light ignite within her heart. Although it was faint, I knew it was possible to create a blaze. "Keep going," I whispered to her heart, encouraging the flame to expand. "You are loved, divinely protected and guided by angels. The whole universe loves you. The whole cosmic collective is cheering you on. We all need you here in it. We want to give you love. Will you open your heart and receive it?"

But Gabriella's face was still in misery. She appeared to be ignoring my voice as she looked to the ground.

"Let's make a garden, and connect with Mother Nature," I said as I handed her some seeds, and together we planted them into the ground.

I called upon the gods of the sun and air, and the goddess of the rain, asking for their blessings—to fertilize the space and enable growth. Gabriella and I stood there together as the rain gently poured down upon us. Then, the sun came out and warmed up the Earth; a gentle breeze kissed the soil. Grass began to grow, overtaking the barren dirt that had once been. Big green trees soon emerged, as the flowers all blossomed, with bright colors of the rainbow. We strolled around the garden, feeling the soft grass beneath our feet and enjoying the smell of sweet perfume tickling our noses. Soon, animals and insects came to say hello. Little fluffy squirrels jumped along the branches and red-chested birds flew by. Butterflies and bees and ladybirds all danced upon the flowers, and the sound of life buzzing with joy-filled our ears.

"Mother Nature will heal your pain and bring you the sacred space you crave. Give your sorrows to her; she will transform your energy into greatness. Everything that she does is for you, because she loves you."

Gabriella slowly looked around her with enchantment. She bent down and smelled the flowers, immersing herself in their beauty. The soft petals caressed her skin and she closed her eyes, feeling the texture and touch of something so profound. The simple smell of nature's perfume gave her the gift to dissociate from her pain. Gabriella was now able to release the madness in her head as she walked amongst nature. She had found a place to belong. She had found a place where she felt safe. She had found a place that brought her great peace as she inhaled its essence. The energy around her was giving her the grounding and nurturing support she needed.

"I am loved by Mother Nature?" she asked. She was showing the first sign of breaking open to love.

"You are loved by the whole universe," I replied, and kissed her forehead.

She sat on the ground and stared with admiration upon the trees and flowers. "I am surrounded by miracles?" she asked.

"Those miracles are within you," I said, feeling pleased with my work.

"I remember who I am," she said. Her soulful heart blazed a flame of pure love from within, shining through the whole space and expanding around us.

I left Gabriella, smiling goodbye. I descended the staircase, realizing I now carried the peace from Gabriella in my heart. When I re-entered my body, I sat with my soul in my sacred space for a little longer. I held myself with love as I reflected on my journey. I sat in my awareness and asked for answers from my soul. *Why this story? Why this day?* I listened as my intuition spoke, telling me I needed to see where the darkness within me came from. It was a message to remind me that my feelings never define me, and that I needed to know how to fix myself. I know the pathway through depressive thoughts and feelings is different for everyone. But for me, I know what I need to do to pave the way forward. I need to use the right tools that remind me of my divine presence in this world. And I do this through the following:

- I need to have a purpose
- I need to believe in a higher power
- I need to connect with Mother Nature.

This is my solution to breathe outside of depression. I remember I am never alone and that I am surrounded by the divine beating heart of creation. These are my gifts to myself to keep me going in times of despair.

Gabriella Reflections

My journey with Gabriella induced many thoughts about my own feelings and where they came from. If the emotions I was feeling currently mirrored the emotions I had endured in a past life, was the energy of my past life still haunting me? And if so, is it her mentality that I tap into when I enter my own dark depression?

So often, I cannot understand where the darkness comes from. I cannot see clearly what is making me feel this way. Even though we are so fortunate to have the mental health resources we do in today's world, I always preferred to succumb to the darkness. There was a strange allurement I felt during those melancholic moments in my life. It was so easy to explore the depth of my emotions whilst finding myself totally absorbed in my misery, holding a strange desperation to feel something, anything. The feeling of numbness would overtake my rationality, and I would go through my day, in this space of grief, while choosing to be ignorant on how to fix myself.

At some point, my depression would eventually take over every area of my life and I would have to pull myself out of it, either through the help of a healer, or by finding purpose in my life and clarity in my day.

When I remembered the truth of my connection to spirit and wholeness with the universe, I dissolved the illusion of separation or loneliness, I found the answers I was seeking. By discovering, and repeatedly experimenting with various spiritual tools, I learned how to shed my depressive thoughts and facilitate my own healing journey.

I wondered if Gabriella also provided me with the strength to overcome my own darkness in this life. Because she had succumbed to misery in her life, perhaps there was a memory of this engraved on my soul's journey? And I would never allow myself to follow the same fate.

Although I was irritated and disappointed that my journey had relayed such depths of sadness, I felt comforted in knowing that I had the power within to create the changes in my life. I couldn't help but marvel at how fascinating it was that my journey through the spirit realm was able to reflect my current needs in addition to revealing a truth and life lesson. Had I not been in a depressed frame of mind, would the vision have made such an impact?

I made a vow to myself to never be like Gabriella again. I would never allow my depression to consume me to the point of madness; I would honor and accept it, but not let it define me. I would make a strong effort to move through it quickly. I was able to apply my optimistic viewpoint to such chaos, but I couldn't disassociate myself from the sadness.

Witnessing Gabriella's life also reminded me that I am fortunate to be living in such a different time. We have an abundance of resources to support mental health in ways like never before. Although the definitions of mental health are blurred, and the list of traits is extensive, there are so many more of us feeling these emotions. We need to reach out to one another, to connect and to learn why this is happening. What is happening in our lives that is creating a world where we feel like we don't belong and we don't connect with each other and Spirit? Do we hold limiting beliefs, forced upon us once upon a time by someone who was also hurting? Are we living in a society that cares more about certain individuals than the collective? I think the answer is yes to all. We need to heal our ancestors' trauma, for it is hovering in our energy field. We need to battle those limiting beliefs and recognize that they do not define us. And most importantly, we need to ignore the mass marketing consumerism behavior that the wealthy shove down our throats. We need to turn off our phones, disconnect from our electronic devices, and get outside more. We keep searching for answers from the internet, when in fact we hold all the answers to the entire universe within us. We need to share those answers with each other and hear each other's stories.

We have the ability to tap into the conscious collective and harness its wisdom. There is an entire web of cosmic energy that connects each and every one of us, and the more we learn how to access that, the more we learn how to trust it, the more power we will gain as we rise together.

The simplest way to find the answers we seek is to understand ourselves, to love ourselves, to nurture ourselves, and to listen to the voice of our soul. The lives that came before us showed the need to quieten our voices and hide our power to survive in the face of the hierarchy. But now, we need to hide ourselves no longer. For we know that equality is the key to world peace. We recognize that this life is ours to harness and live as we choose. We are only as small as we believe ourselves to be, and, likewise, we can become as great and almighty as we choose. We cannot continue to live in fear of others. We need to be ourselves, love ourselves, and respect ourselves. That same kindness, compassion, love, and respect that we give to ourselves, needs to be shared with everyone around us. And the more we learn how to do this, the more we educate each other by leading by example. The more we choose to be this way, the more connected we will feel, the more liberated we will be, and the easier our lives will flow.

Georgiana

Georgiana

Over the next few days, I allocated time to myself to focus on my self-care and self-love routine. Although I know the routine that works for me, I also know that it's important to change it up to keep it interesting. I started to incorporate a morning walk into my day, and I noticed a big difference in my attitude. No longer was I depressed in the cold, dark winter. I transformed my mind by connecting with nature, and choosing to see the beauty in seasonal changes.

When the time came to journey again, I was sure to cleanse my energy thoroughly before and after. I incorporated this practice into my meditation. I would imagine an opening in the ground before me, and I would envision any stuck energy falling down into the hole. This included any negative thoughts or fears, or any preconceived ideas of what I wanted to happen; I would give those energies to the Earth. Once they fell into that space, I sent them love and let them know they weren't needed. I would then imagine a beautiful silver waterfall above me, coming down from the sky. This waterfall would cleanse me and fill me up with blissful cosmic energy of pure love and light. I was giving and receiving energy at the same time, and I trusted that I was protected, safe, and supported. Then, I would commence my ritual.

When I arrived at the top of the stairs of the upper world during this journey, the king and queen were standing there waiting for me. I noticed that I was now wearing an unusually long gray dress in a soft fabric. Instead of being escorted to the path on the right or left, their majesties encouraged me to walk straight between them. I followed their request and a new pathway appeared.

As I walked along the path I asked, "Is this a past life or ancestry?"

"Both," was the queen's response. "You are visiting one of your own past lives of your current bloodline."

I followed the path until a circular window appeared in front of me. I opened the glass and stepped through, arriving at a grand bedroom. There were high ceilings and lavish curtains covering the windows. There was a piano in the corner, and a lovely balcony that overlooked a forest that stretched out as far as I could see. I could tell that I was living in an extremely luxurious house in this life, but I felt completely alone. I walked outside to the edge of the balcony and looked down to see a stone floor with large potted plants below. There was a small boy, perhaps no older than eight, dressed in a suit. He was playing with a piece of string attached to a wooden stick. I waved and smiled and went down to meet him.

He gave me a big hug. "Mummy," he said, and cuddled into my skirts.

A younger woman in a uniform appeared on the patio. "Shall I attend to Master Thomas's lunch, Missus Georgiana?"

I nodded in approval. The two of them went into the house and left me to walk around the grounds. I searched for recognition of something. But all I found was sadness being this woman. There was something missing from this life; Georgiana desired change, and wanted to search for something more, but didn't have the confidence to leave the palatial prison.

I saw a water fountain and walked over to it, to see my reflection. As I peered over the edge, I saw a strikingly beautiful woman of about 40, dark blue-gray eyes and long, fiery red hair in tight ringlets. I appeared very soft and gentle, yet I couldn't connect entirely to this woman. As I continued to stare at my reflection, I found myself merging with Georgiana's body even deeper. I was taking on the role of my past life in finer detail. It was similar to how it felt with Selina, only that, unlike Selina, I did not feel uneasy with the energy Georgiana possessed. Georgiana was weak. And I felt like she had spent many years living this way.

As I looked at her face in the water, her story played out before me; she told me what had become of her life. Georgiana had security, a family, wealth, and safety. The house was her inheritance, not that of a husband. She had been fortunate to be born into a long line of wealth, and I wondered if perhaps this had started from Bonita, for it was the same bloodline. Georgiana had been an only child. I could feel the power she had as a woman with great wealth, yet she had nowhere to explore that power. Georgiana was terribly lonely. Her husband was never around, always "working," but he didn't need the money, it was more of an act to prove he was worthy of her riches. Her husband hated the townsfolk gossiping that he didn't deserve her. But none of this mattered to Georgiana. She just wanted to feel passion and peace.

"I want to show you something," Georgiana said in the reflection, as her eyes turned a darker gray. I found myself separating from her body. I was taking on the role of the observer.

Georgiana led me toward the forest next to her home. I felt as though she liked to come here often and watch the world around her home from afar. She took me to a large rock protruding from the ground; it had a ring of medium-sized oak trees around it.

REMEMBER THE WITCH WITHIN

"This is my favorite place in the whole world," Georgiana said as she kneeled on the ground next to the stone and placed her hand on it. She closed her eyes. "I don't feel like I belong in this world. Something is missing, and this stone, this forest, is the only place that makes me feel alive."

Georgiana opened her eyes and stood up. She hovered over the stone. She took a small bone knife out of her pocket and pricked the base of her palm while holding it over the stone.

"I don't know why I do this, but I feel compelled to," she said as she watched a speck of blood drip from her hand onto the stone. "I feel like I can hear a heart beating loudly when my blood touches the rock, like they are connected somehow, in someway. But I have no one to show me, I have no one to tell me why I do the things I do. I just know there is something here for me."

Georgiana sat down and leaned her back against the stone. She cocked her head to one side as she looked over to her house to see if anyone was watching.

"I feel nothing when I look at my home. I feel as empty as those rooms. I know it is shameful to say this, for I have the kind of security that many people only dream about. But, I don't feel seen, I don't feel heard." She wept, and I could feel her misery as she struggled to accept her life. "This is the only place I have ever felt truly alive." She rubbed her hand over the rock, caressing the rough surface, the white rubble and black dirt. She slid her hand down to the base where the rock protruded from the earth.

Georgiana dug around the base of the rock with her dainty hands, deep into the ground. Her nails were filled with dirt and I could hear the rubble scratching against the rock as she desperately poked around it. She was searching for something only she knew existed. Her heart told her there was something there, and she held hope that whatever she discovered would bring her the enlightenment she craved. So her hands scraped and dug deeper. But the stone was buried too deeply. It was connected to the crust of the earth and it would be impossible to find its beginning. I wanted to tell her that the answers were within her, that she had the power to seek the connection with the spirit world through her own inner self. But my voice held no sound; I couldn't get through to her.

As I watched Georgiana desperately try to reach the bottom of the stone, I couldn't help but think of it as a metaphor for her life. The outside of the rock was the facade that she presented to the world. But deep below the surface where no one could see, the rock was connected to the great force of energy, to the source of creation, just like she was. She only knew her persona, that which she portrayed due to the social class that she was born into. She was only familiar with the version of herself that was acceptable in her reality. Yet she craved to dive deep and reach the other side—a side of herself that was hidden from the world and even to her. She craved answers to her questions of who she was and why she was on this Earth.

Georgiana continued to dig until her hands disappeared from view. She left them there in the dirt for a few moments, feeling the energy that pulsated beneath her. She had found a moment of connection and familiarity.

"This is the only place I have ever felt truly alive," she repeated. Then she showed me some of the ways she used the space. A vision of Georgiana riding a horse naked under the moonlight came forth to me. Her hair was a crazed mess of red curls, and her eyes were alive, yet drunk with madness. She was exhilarated. Rain poured down harshly around her as the sound of thunder engulfed our ears. She jumped off the horse and stood upon the stone. Waving her hands wildly up high in the sky, she harnessed the energy of the lightning above her. She didn't know what she was doing or why she was doing it, but she didn't care. She felt like she finally belonged. There, in the dark, beneath the moonlight, where no one could see, she was finally free to be herself without any judgment.

"I should love being in my home with my family, but out here in nature is where I feel true love." Georgiana sighed and looked to the ground. "I've tried to bring others here, but no one connects with it the same way I do. I told a lady in the village about it, but she hushed me. She told me to never tell anyone that I hold this passion for the forest. She said it would bring great shame upon my family. So, I've kept my passion hidden."

I sat down with Georgiana by the stone and reflected on her pain. The disconnection she felt from the real world felt similar to the feelings I'd had as a child. The undeniable feeling of being different, feeling like no one knew what I was going through, and that no one had the same feelings as me. I knew loneliness far too well. It had suffocated me for most of my childhood and early adult life. But fortunately, in my late 20s, I started to understand my spiritual side and reveal my own power. I was able to nurture that voice within, able to learn what I needed to know and I trusted that intuition as it guided me to create my own rituals.

But here was Georgiana, sad, alone and confused, with no one to talk to. I could feel myself embodying her sadness, feeling that her life was a downward spiral, a drowning place that only enabled her to survive through a tiny opening of fresh air. I wasn't sure how I could help her, or what else I was to learn if anything other than just my own empathy. I began to be consumed with her pain and confusion. It felt as though she really had nowhere to go, no opportunity, no possibilities. As the weaker sex, she was stuck in a position of submissiveness, with no one to talk with who understood her pain.

But, I did not wish to fall down in despair, and so I set my intention once more, speaking out to my spirit guides, asking what more I was to learn in this life as Georgiana.

Georgiana II

My spirit guides answered my request instantly, and I found myself walking hurriedly behind Georgiana. She was dressed in ragged clothes and appeared to have aged about fifteen years. She walked quickly through the town center, oblivious to the glances directed at her; it was obvious she didn't entirely fit in with the common folk. Despite the faded scarf wrapped around her head, locks of clean vibrant red hair escaped. And, although she had rubbed her face with ashes and dirt, it didn't match the villagers' true peasant attire from having gone months without washing. Georgiana's fresh, perfumed scent gave away her disguise. Still, it didn't deter her, for she had a mission. She kept her head down as she walked toward her destination.

The streets were narrow and were lined with washing —sheets, and clothes—hanging from the windows to dry. People sat about idly. A handful of market stalls were scattered in front of the villagers' homes. There was no distinction between home and work; they lived and breathed the two together.

Many people continued to look at Georgiana as she bustled by with her head down, knowing the way as though by memory. The streets smelled of filth. But Georgiana was unfazed, she continued to weave through the village with confidence. The contrast to her own life reminded Georgiana to feel deep gratitude for the support, security, and safety she had been born into. Although she wanted deeper meaning in her life, she knew she wouldn't survive if she were to give up her luxuries. She didn't wish to be in a different situation, but she did wish for peace in her thoughts, and for answers to her questions. She craved a soulful connection with someone who shared the same viewpoints as her.

Georgiana finally stopped at the end of an alleyway and walked through a house, that connected through to another house, and then into a small room, where an old lady was sitting. Georgiana greeted her warmly and opened up a basket that she had been carrying. She placed its contents on the table.

"I brought you today's bread and raspberry jam," Georgiana said, as the smell of fresh bread wafted through the room. "I had some this morning, it was delicious. I thought that you would like it."

"Thank you, dear, you are very kind," the old lady said as she patted the table to find the bread. It was here that I knew she was blind.

"I had another strange dream last night, Beatrice," Georgiana said pacing around the room with excitement.

"And, what was your intention, before you went to sleep?"

"To be shown the afterlife," Georgiana sighed. "I don't believe that there is nothing. I don't agree with the church doctrine. I cannot keep pretending that I do." She threw her hands up in the air with frustration as she shook her head vigorously.

"But you must, dear. I have told you this before. You cannot speak of what must remain unspoken. Many have come before you, and many of them no longer stand because they spoke their thoughts out loud."

Georgiana kneeled before Beatrice and held her hands. The old lady rubbed them gently in a caring manner.

"But I need something more in my life," Georgiana said. "I want to learn more about the magic. I want to learn more about the powers of what I cannot see. I want to learn what happens after we die."

"Hush my dear, you will learn all of this."

"I will?"

REMEMBER THE WITCH WITHIN

"Yes, you will. Because you want to. Everything you want to know is coming to you."

"I am ready. I am open. I promise," Georgiana begged.

"Then, let us begin," Beatrice replied, pointing toward an old chest in the corner of the room.

Georgiana walked over to the chest, opened it up, and pulled out a small box. She brought it over to the table and gave it to Beatrice. Georgiana moved easily like she had done this many times before. I realized she must have been seeing Beatrice in secret for a long time. I asked my guides how they knew each other.

It was common for the wealthy to distribute food to the widows and disabled. One day, while offering food to the poor, Georgiana met Beatrice. When Beatrice told Georgiana that her energy felt troubled, it caught her attention. No one had ever spoken to her so frankly before. Beatrice explained how Georgiana could calm herself with the vibrations of the earth, and from there, the conversation flowed. Georgiana's favorite day of the week was visiting Beatrice and learning from her. As their friendship blossomed, Georgiana felt safe to share her connection with her special rock. In exchange, Beatrice foretold a secret spell for Georgiana to ignite power from that rock. And when Georgiana followed Beatrice's instructions, she felt an instant change within her essence. A whole new world of feelings and emotions expanded from her body, in ways that she didn't even know possible. She continued to visit Beatrice for more guidance after that experience. Being that Beatrice was blind, she would never be able to identify Georgiana as someone acting unlawfully or exploring witchcraft. And so, Beatrice became Georgiana's first-ever true friend.

"Now dear, hidden behind the chest there is a brown bag tied with string. Bring it to me."

Georgiana did as she was told and carried the small bag over to Beatrice.

"What is it?" Georgiana asked as she sat down next to her.

"I was given this by a friend from the north. Open it."

Georgiana unraveled the string and opened up the brown cloth to find a black onyx crystal and three runes. Her eyes twinkled with excitement. "They are beautiful! What are they?"

"They will protect you and help open up your connection with the spirit world," Beatrice said as she pushed the crystal toward Georgiana. "This black one, it's an onyx. It will keep away evil. When you go home, bury this stone into the ground in front of your door. Very deep. As you bury it, speak with the spirits. Ask them for protection, ask them to keep you safe. No one can know you have this or see you burying it."

"I will, thank you," Georgiana replied, holding the black stone tightly and closing her eyes.

"And the runes here will spark magic from above. I will show you how to use them. But first, promise me that you will hide these with the others I've given you."

"I will," Georgiana replied and kissed the old lady's hands in gratitude.

My vision flashed over to see Georgiana back in her home. She was standing by the window removing a piece of wood from the wall. She retrieved a small box from the cubbyhole and opened it proudly. Inside the box was a small scroll, a piece of bone, some feathers, some herbs, and a string. That box contained all the secrets she had been keeping since meeting Beatrice, and it was her most prized possession. She quickly placed the runes with them and returned the box to its hiding place.

My vision returned to Beatrice as she continued the conversation. "Too many people have been tortured.

You cannot trust anyone. There will come a time when we can speak freely but now is not the time. There are too many changes taking place in the world. We must act in secret for the time being. Even if you think you can tell someone about this, you cannot. Your staff must never know."

"I know, I know. It is safe, it is secret. It is sacred," Georgiana replied, only now I could feel she had more confidence in her voice.

"Shall we begin?" Beatrice asked.

"Yes."

Georgiana sat down next to Beatrice as the two held hands and closed their eyes. Beatrice spoke a language I had not heard before, and the two softly chanted together harmoniously. They used their hands and mouths to create a sound journey that allowed their souls to transcend through the infinite layer of space and time. Beatrice guided Georgiana through the unseen realms as they met with their spirit guides, their angels, and whoever else that they wished to summon for support and advice. The energy they created together transformed into vibrant neon colors. Those lights continued to evolve into sacred geometrical patterns, flowing and shifting, and dancing amidst the energy between them. As I watched them, the magic they had created resonated through me, reminding me of my deep connection with the universe.

When the two women shared time together they had not a care in the world. A protective layer of cosmic energy enveloped them. It descended from the heavens as they conversed in secret whispers. For the first time in Georgiana's life, she had a soulful connection, she finally felt seen and heard. She never wanted that feeling to leave. But like everything in this world, change is inevitable.

One day, when Georgiana returned to visit Beatrice, she was there no longer. She couldn't dare ask the villagers what had happened to her, whether she had passed, or whether she had been caught. Whatever happened, Georgiana knew she must never return to find out, for Beatrice had made her promise. And so she never did.

Shortly afterward, Georgiana fired all of her staff. Her husband eventually passed over and she learned how to take care of herself, although this behavior in itself was deemed inappropriate and she was rumored to be unwell. Her son still visited her, caring for her until her last days. But he never knew the truth of what had happened to her or why she had entered this solitary way of life. She never handed over her wisdom or knowledge of the universe to him.

My vision changed one last time. Georgiana and I stood together again on her balcony, overlooking her garden. Many years would have passed by now, and her red curls had turned grey. But, most importantly, the energy of her soul had changed. A great depth of transformation had taken place. She had completely evolved from a shy, insecure woman who hid behind the stone to worship her earth in the early hours of the morning unseen, to a bold woman who performed ritual magic without caring about doing it "right." She still practiced magic alone in the forest. She still had no one to share her visions with, and it was still too dangerous for her to speak of her desires and practices. But I could see the increase in her inner power and the unbreakable bond she had developed with the spirit world. She may not have known exactly what she was doing, but she knew that it made her feel good. By allowing her actions to roam freely, she had managed to break herself out of her glass prison. Her ability to act upon her instincts had provided her with the peace and answers she had been seeking. Her transcendental meditative state of consciousness gave her the strength to carry on.

Georgiana raised her hands up high to the sky, and I watched her wild mess of gray curls bounce around

REMEMBER THE WITCH WITHIN

her head. In front of us were specks of rainbow light flickering in the sky. And I could see and feel the energy of other spirits nearby. She had conjured them, she had discovered the secret to thinning the veil between her and the spirit world. She had gathered wisdom, magic, and power. But how?

"In my dreams," she replied, hearing my thoughts. "I was shown the truth of my soul. I saw the transition of my soul move through my conscious awakening into the space of the unseen. My dreams allowed me to explore those realms without my mind taking control and translating them. I always knew there were two worlds, I just didn't know what that really meant, or how they worked together. But from my need to visit that rock, that sacred space of earth, I finally managed to find the gateway between the two worlds. And, as time went on, and my practices became stronger, I was able to open that gateway on my own and build a bridge between them."

I left Georgiana's world with peace in my heart. And, as I opened my eyes, I felt as though my power had grown too. The determination that Georgiana held to never give up, to continue following her passions despite the rest of the world telling her not to, gave me strength. And even though she told me that the secrets of spiritual wisdom had died with her, the power of stepping into her truth ignited ripples in the future bloodline. And this inspiration to encourage others to be themselves was then engraved in the conscious collective, waiting to be retrieved by another soul, at another time, in another life.

Reiko

Reiko

Like all spiritual practices, the more I repeated my ritual, the greater my connection with the spirit world became. And the more my inner strength erupted. With each journey, my visions became clearer and amplified with fine details. I found myself being drawn deeper into the journey, eager to learn more. The next time I journeyed, I was taken to another past life. But as I walked along the left pathway of the king and queen, I was ushered down below into my lower world.

I knew it was my lower world because I see the same entrance to that world every time I journey below, regardless of the intention. The entrance has a stairway of thick mud. The base landing is completely surrounded by trees, and a narrow path leads me to a small opening where there is a river. Often, I would stand at this river as a wooden raft pulled up to take me somewhere. Other times, my spirit animal, the crocodile, would be waiting for me, and I usually sat upon his back.

Today, there was a beautiful Japanese lady waiting for me by the river, as a bamboo raft pulled up. She looked at me. Her expression was solemn, yet there was a deep peace behind it. Her face was painted with white powder, and her black hair was drawn back into a tight low bun. She wore a white and green kimono and tiny red slippers.

"You can call me Reiko," she said, as though reading my mind.

I sat behind Reiko on the bamboo raft and we moved along the river channel. I looked into the water and saw the eyes of my crocodile appear. He was swimming alongside us, bobbing his head along with his beady eyes poking out of the water. I felt safe just seeing him. My crocodile is with me in the lower world every time I visit. I say he is my spirit animal, but he could very well be a spirit guide that manifests as a crocodile. The important thing is, I know I can rely on him for strength, wisdom, and care.

Reiko and I floated along the water, slowly and gracefully. Each pocket of riverbank that opened up at the edge of the forest held a different scene of people living their lives. There were some children bathing in the water, giggling and splashing. Another scene showed a group of mothers washing clothes in the river. There was also a couple in love, sitting on the riverbank and holding hands. Although a few people looked up at us, our presence on the water phased no one; together we lived in harmony.

Reiko and I traveled along this river for a long time, until we finally reached what felt like the end. The wooden raft pulled up to the riverbank and we got out. We walked through a rainforest where low branches hung from enormous trees, and the smell of mud permeated the air. I loved being surrounded by an abundance of nature. We reached a wall of hanging vines; Reiko lifted them up and an opening appeared, revealing a large, ancient Japanese pagoda.

The pagoda was painted white and had wooden carvings around the edges of the roof. It had an immaculate Japanese garden decorating the entranceway. We walked into the pagoda, and inside I was greeted by an old man, probably in his late 80s, wearing a white robe. He had a long white mustache and he was sitting cross-legged on a small rug. There were two small rugs laid out on the ground in front of him. Reiko motioned for me to sit down on one of them. The old man smiled as I did so. It was a warm-hearted smile like we were old friends, like he had been waiting for me. At this point, I felt my body and Reiko's interchange: I became her, then separated. It was a signal to show me that I had once been her. This was my past life as Reiko.

"This is Ku," Reiko said. She bowed down and I followed.

I felt an overpowering sensation of deep respect for Ku as I bowed before him. Even though I had no recollection of my life as Reiko, nor knew what Ku meant to her (me), I knew there was something incredibly profound about his energetic presence. I wanted to learn more. Although I sat there as a student, I felt equal. It was as though I had already mastered the lessons he would teach me during a previous life, and I was there to remember. I felt like I had the answers already. I felt at peace.

"Thank you, Ku," I said in response, eager to learn what was to become of this experience.

But he did not speak. Instead, we just sat there in silence, in stillness.

I looked to Reiko who looked to me and back to Ku. Ku was looking at no one. He continued to gaze softly, a few feet in front of his body. His breathing began to slow down as he entered a meditative state. I proceeded to follow his behavior and when I had slowed my vibration down to meet him, did his voice become clear to me. And together, we communicated through this channel.

"I know your pathway," he said, as a deep drumming voice came through in my head. "You are here to remember. In your previous lives, you have learned how to harness the energy outside of you. You have connected with the universal energies around you. You have felt their vibrations above and below, and you've learned how those vibrations can move you. Now, I will teach you that it all starts from within. This life that you had as Reiko, was purely to learn how to master that stillness. You never left this space. You stayed with me all of your life to learn the wisdom from silence."

A vision of Reiko's life played out before me. She had been abandoned as a child. I saw being about three years old, crying in an alley with garbage all around her. She had grown up on the streets, and developed rage and hate in her heart. But she was determined to change. She wanted to find out why it had happened. Why she lived that way. Why she had grown up without her parents. She heard of Ku's place from the villagers. It sounded safe there. She needed safety. She arrived at age sixteen and never left.

"Follow me as we journey within," Ku continued, bringing my attention back to our seated position. My essence interwove with Reiko's as she sat beside me; I felt her energy and support for this journey.

As directed by Ku, I followed his lead, and turned my focus inwards. I was meditating within my own meditative journey, and what I revealed brought great enlightenment to my waking life. For he took me deep within my own imagination. And upon doing so, my mind peeled away to a point of non-existence. Deeper and deeper my inner realm expanded, as the layers of this perceived reality, and my projected cosmic world, melted, revealing an opening of space that could not be explained, it could only be felt. Within this understanding was a divine feeling of pure bliss, of connection and unity, of wholeness and love. It was high vibrational energy, it felt like I had ascended through the realms of consciousness, and passed over into nirvana.

The vision dispersed into a blank landscape and together, as two souls of spirit light, we journeyed through the realms of internal bliss. The landscape morphed into a galaxy of infinite stars; despite the inability to see, I knew that it was the most vast space I had ever encountered.

I already knew the universe was limitless, but what I was learning was that this limitless was also within me. I too bore the identity of a bountiful place to discover, a space that held no boundaries, and enveloped the depth of beauty, truth, and lightness that the universe mirrored. My physical matter held definitions of its capabilities, but the definitions evolved, transforming according to my own awareness. But in this space, I held no preconceived ideas, no philosophical terminologies to attempt to explain; I simply felt my sensations and allowed them to tell me the true pathway forward.

Ku continued to explain the connections together: as above, so below; as within, so without. He showed me with imagery how my own internal world reflects the outside world around me, and that it always starts from within. My visualizations started in my core, from the light of my soul, and expanded to create the reality before me. The imagery danced back and forth, showing the patterns that interlaced the veil of the two worlds—my soul and the Universe. The internal and external. As the dance between the two grew with passion and strength, I saw that the line was blurred, that it only existed in my mind, for we were as one. And I realized the most important lesson of all of my life.

The Universe is within me.

My soul is cosmic intelligence. I am connected to all of source energy. And that same source energy that creates the whole universe, also creates me. It always starts with me. All this time, I had spent in my waking life asking the spirits for guidance, love, and support, thinking they were outside of me, only to learn the answers were always within me. I created those answers just as I created the questions. My decisions and creations reflected my universe. Not the other way around. I'd once assumed my life flowed according to the universe's time, but I now knew the opposite was true. It was an impactful lesson, learned through the simplest of tools—meditation. I had explored meditation throughout my life, but this was a new venture. I no longer saw myself separate from love or from others or from the world. I saw myself right smack in the middle. I saw myself as the entry point to the world around me, and from this entry point, I was able to influence my life. I was able to perceive and understand my life. I no longer saw the divine as an energy outside of me. Rather, I was the divine source creating the universe around me.

Reiko II

My journey with Reiko and Ku led to a great awakening within me. One that is usually only attained through overcoming great trauma or a sharp change of perception forced by outside actions. But here, I was, able to alter my perception of my world through my own internal magical vibrations. I wasn't relying on another's actions, I was creating those actions within me, and, bit by bit, my perception was cracking open. But just how deeply could that opening be broken? How easily could I move my awareness over to the other side to see the truth around me? I craved to hold on to this understanding, but as soon as I left the lower world, my interpretation became much harder to grasp. There was a mental block. The tighter I tried to hold onto my new outlook, the quicker it left me. I realized that the only way I could keep this new perception was to trust my knowing, my power of divinity, and not try to comprehend it, to explain it. I would simply become it, and let that truth embody me.

I went through my daily life as normal after this experience, but something had shifted within me. Something I couldn't quite comprehend. I felt more powerful and confident. I felt almost addicted to the other worlds, I wanted to see what else I could see, and learn what else needed to be learned. So, I entered my ritual again, setting the intention to return to the life of Reiko.

I arrived in the lower world through the muddy path and was met by Reiko again. She was standing on the raft at the river waiting for me. We floated along the water and arrived at the hanging vines that hid the entrance to the Japanese pagoda. When we walked through the entrance, Ku was already waiting for us and he was standing in front of a large tree. My inclination was to walk over to him and bow, but when I did, he didn't respond. He was unfazed, and I felt as though I had never left him. Perhaps we were simply continuing our previous encounter together. This recognition prompted me to wonder: *Does my soul continue to live on in these realms without my conscious awareness?*

It's impossible to truly comprehend the unlimited power of my soul, for to define such energy would be to create boundaries, and creating boundaries suggests a limit. That is not the truth of our soul. Our soul is the most intelligent, wisest, purest form of loving light energy that exists; it holds unlimited possibilities. So, to live in another time, in another realm as me, but not as me, could very well be true.

I looked to Ku, wanting to hear the answers to my questions. But he only pointed to the tree that reached up high into the clouds.

"You are the same as the tree," he said, opening up his hands and directing them toward me and the tree. "You have a heartbeat like the tree, you have roots that sink deep into the ground, and those roots are fed by Mother Nature. This nurturing food provides you with balance and harmony. You have emotions and needs just like the tree does. You grow together, with water and sunlight. This tree was created from a seed, it has ancestors just like you. You are the tree. Work on removing the dissociation that you feel between the two, and allow yourself to merge with the tree."

Ku walked closer to the tree and motioned for me to do the same. He placed his hand upon the tree trunk, to which I followed. I felt myself morph into the cosmic perception of the tree and become its energy. Our energies were merging with each other, yet remained separate. I was in unity and yet completely separate.

"Here, feel its heartbeat. Come closer and hold it tightly. Allow your energy to swirl together. You are becoming the tree. There is great wisdom to be learned from the tree."

As I allowed my energy to replicate the heartbeat of the tree, I felt pleasurable peace overwhelm my senses.

"This is the tree's energy," Ku continued, as his voice in my ear grew louder. "See its spirit."

I focused my attention on the frame of the tree as the most wonderful vision of spirit energy came through to me, telling me it was the angelic spirit of the tree.

"You are no better than the tree," Ku said. "We are all equal. We are the same level, the same power, the same creation. No one, no thing is superior." The image of the tree's spirit faded away and I found myself falling amidst the realm of unconsciousness once more, into the pure darkness of unlimited potential.

I stood in this bliss for several minutes, allowing my energy to be filled up completely with nurturing love until I heard a voice in my ear, it was that of Ku. He had not left me, he was still speaking as my teacher.

"You are the water too," Ku said, as he stood in front of a babbling brook. The water was flowing effortlessly over smooth fist-sized stones. "The water reflects the flow of energy in your body. You are water too. But sometimes, you hold yourself back. See the stones?" He picked up a stone and then another and started to pile them up high. "See what's happening now?" he asked rhetorically. The stones towered over the stream, restricting the flow.

"The water is unable to move easily, you see? The rocks are impeding the current. The water has to move around it. It still flows, but there's resistance, it has to change direction." He pointed to the areas that were stopping the water. "Find the resistance within you, find what is holding you back from being yourself."

Ku picked up more stones and started piling them up in various places, continuing to prove his point. "We are now starting to create more blockages here, we are interfering with the natural flow of energy. The longer we leave the blockages, the more concrete they become. Our natural energetic flow is changing. One who has many towers has more work to do, but they can still work through them. There is no limit to how much one can heal."

"What if someone is tired of working through these blockages all the time?" I asked wondering how many towers of stones were impeding my life.

"These blockages may have accumulated from past lives, from our ancestors, or they can be from present lives. There are lots of reasons for them to exist. But they are simply energy. They are energy manifested into consciousness, arising from negative thoughts, false and limiting beliefs, traumatic events, shame, guilt, or hurt. They are conscious thoughts of energy that have transformed into blockages and cause us harm and disease. Enter through those blockages, move through the resistance within you, and, with time, your energy will flow more beautifully, more gracefully. Each time a wall is broken down, the water flows faster. It flows stronger with more power. That is what will happen to you if you move through your pain. This is where you will go if you choose to rid yourself of everything holding you back from being true to yourself. The only thing in your way is yourself."

Ku dismantled each of the rock piles slowly, showing how the direct flow returned once the barriers were removed. As I watched the release in front of me, I felt the same release inside me. A harmonic resonance emerged within and I found myself relaxing a little bit deeper.

"Let me show you the mountain." Ku's voice echoed in my mind again as the scenery changed. We were now sitting on top of a mountain. The horizon expanded far and wide. I could see snow-frosted tips on the mountains below. And dense forests with rivers running through them. The air lifted beneath us as the sun set in the distance. The moon rose and the stars sprinkled then disappeared, as the sun rose again. We watched this cycle repeat in a harmonious circle, signifying the passing of days.

"Every day, we honor the sun. We give gratitude for its blessings, its fire, its warmth, light, and wisdom. It gives us life. Allow your own energy to be in alignment with the rhythms of the sun and the moon. Everything in your world is connected to a rhythmic cycle, but you need to find that cycle for yourself. We are similar but unique. Although our days may appear to have the same cyclic melody replaying, there are changes. There is creation, destruction, and transformation. It is an evolving pattern of beauty that enables profound growth to be revealed within each cycle. You are simply learning the same lesson but unraveling deeper truths. When the lesson and the wisdom disperse, then you will become completely as one with the universe."

The visions repeated themselves, showing me the cycle of energies that they possessed. Creation, destruction, and transformation replayed over and over again. I could see the impact the solar system has on Earth as the seasons emerged and dispersed with each day and year. As I watched dusk turn to dawn, cold becomes hot, snow and rain fall, and the life cycles of animals, I felt myself reflect those same changes. It represented the truth that Ku had been explaining—that I was at the heart of the whole of creation, and our cycles were synchronized.

"How did you come to understand this?" I asked Ku.

"I studied nature. I spent days and nights living with nature through the seasons. Even in the freezing cold, I stayed immersed in nature and listened to what it had to say. The trees shared their knowledge of the Earth with me. The wind whispered the truth of consciousness to me. And the energy of the universe moved through me."

I asked my guides what had become of Reiko and her life with Ku. Their story played out before me. They lived like father and daughter through the rest of their lives. Reiko mastered the lesson of what it meant to exist beyond the physical realm. She spent days and nights living in the forest next to the comfort of Ku's home, by choice. He taught her what the true energy of her soul meant. She would wander among the trees, connecting to the Earth and learning from spirit. She was never scared, and never felt alone. And from this process, the rage within her heart melted away. Finally, she had found the safety she sought through the love of Mother Nature, and her search for answers about her family never resurfaced. She found great meaning in her life from living off the Earth and learning from Ku.

I saw Ku die. I saw Reiko bury him. I saw his body being left in the woods for nature to take it. He didn't believe his body belonged to him, it was part of the ecosystem, so he had requested it to be given back to nature. Reiko did just that. She took over the work of the temple, but she stayed humble. Many visitors came to visit but no one stayed. Reiko bore no children, she had no family. But she had developed the most profound wisdom through the work of Ku, and that depth of connection and understanding lived on through the web of the collective unconsciousness, ready to be harnessed by anyone who wished to do so.

Margaret

Margaret

I felt an unbreakable bond to my past lives. I was finding deep change within me from exploring these stories, for they held not only the wisdom of spiritual awareness, but of the ability to survive and thrive as a woman. But I still had questions and doubts as to whether these lives would hold as much importance to others as they did to me. It's like any creative process, there are always doubts. *Am I learning what is needed to be known? Am I sharing wisdom of importance with the world?* Just when I felt like giving up, I determinedly chose to push through and keep going, waiting for that breakthrough moment when all of the pieces fit together. The moment when it would become clear that I was following the right path.

I felt like there was a life missing from my story. I had one more I needed to reveal. So I journeyed to the unseen realms with the intention of asking who else I needed to meet. As I walked to the upper world, the king and queen were standing at the top of the stairs once more. I was pleased to see them again—even though I never expected them or asked them to be there, they just always were. Always in different positions, but always there, as an anchor to my journeying. I felt supported and heard.

They moved apart, displaying the entrance behind them; I felt my energy being pulled toward it. I recognized this pathway from before; this was the entry point to both my own past life and that of my bloodline.

The pathway turned into a pale-colored dirt path, with large trees growing on either side, as though planted on purpose by man. I continued to walk until I arrived at a large green hedge. As I peeked through I could see an opening. There was a woman standing there, looking out to the garden.

"Margaret." I heard, as I walked closer to her. Margaret was her name.

She directed me to walk toward the house where a small table and two chairs were set up waiting for us. An ornate Chinese teapot and delicately painted teacups were laid out for us. We sat down and looked out into the garden. There was complete stillness, with the simplicity of the present moment, just watching the world float by. I loved the silence, the beauty of the landscape before me and the simplistic moment of sharing time with another. But, of course, I wasn't there to absorb the landscape. I knew Margaret had a story for me, so I asked her what had become of her life. Why was it important for me to meet her?

"This is when everything changed," Margaret said. "Women no longer feel inferior to men. We are learning the importance of stepping into our power. Although still, we need to do so carefully, for our timing must be impeccable."

I could see the vision of Margaret's life as she carried on throughout her day. Her tasks were easy, such as choosing which tablecloth to use, what food the family would eat, and what flowers to bring into the house. She didn't have to make any serious decisions other than what went on in the household. She managed her staff, she supported her children, and she was loyal to her husband, but that was the extent of her tasks. Five children appeared before me, showing that she had fulfilled her duty of bearing children, and she enveloped them with all of the love possible.

"Love is the secret to gaining the power back. I understood my worth." As she spoke, a vision flashed to see Margaret looking into a mirror in her bedroom. "I understood the power of the female. The power of choice and choosing who I wanted to be. I learned how to manage people, how to smile at my husband and get my way."

"It sounds like manipulation," I suggested, although I really knew nothing of the challenges she faced.

"I learned to gain power through understanding myself and learning how others perceived me," she said. "Power is gained through knowledge, awareness, and by seeing the truth of the world. Power is gained by truly understanding people."

My vision moved over to a lavish dinner party being hosted by Margaret and her husband. She wore a long crimson dress, heavily decorated with beads and lace. The skirt was full and padded and the style of it reminded me of some time in the Victorian era. Her hair was fastened up high, and she carried a small lace fan, used to shield her eyes when peering at another. She led me through the room as though I were a guest, and I followed her lead graciously. The vision of the other guests was blurred, but there was vibrant energy; it was obvious that there were many people around us.

I determined that we were living at a time when women were still oppressed. Margaret's husband sat at the head of the table, although Margaret's strong character made me think she was actually the head of the household. There was something daring about the confidence of Margaret. The way she presented herself; she was charismatic yet refrained from being too indulgent with another. She preferred to sit back and observe silently but, as a lady of the upper class, she had to be presentable and live according to society's rules. She was a respectful host, always kind to her guests and happy to converse, but she cared more about those around her and the way people presented themselves to the world. Margaret had an intriguing personality; one that came from a deep understanding of the world around her.

I watched as Margaret swooned over her friends. It seemed she concealed her true self while pretending to be as they wanted her to be. When I questioned her about it, she laughed, responding with vague questions about the concept of reality.

"This is my role in life, to host and be a mother, both of which require me to wait on others. Never for myself. Who I choose to portray to others is how I make it, so why not make it fun? I'm not hurting anyone by playing out different versions of myself, I'm just learning how to breathe as me. Each of these layers I show them, are still a part of me." Margaret leaned in closer to me as she spoke. I could see her beauty clearly. Her striking black eyes were full of mischief yet sincerity. I wanted to tell her all of my thoughts and secrets, knowing that those eyes were a vault of mystery, and exclusivity. And, had I been a stranger in this past life I would have done so, but I now knew that the exchange of secrets would not have been even. For Margaret was quite reserved, despite the safety and trust she exuded, allowing others to be themselves.

Perhaps that was her gift—she created a safe space for another to explore their soul. She had a charismatic charm that enabled her to extract information. That was her power, as she said—to transform that information into a profound understanding of her perception of life. She gained her wisdom this way. I watched her carefully choose which dinner guest to attend to. Once chosen, Margaret's behavior was bewitching. She would perform her charms with precision, learning about their thoughts and secrets ever so cleverly. Her mind was calculating everyone's movements; observing and analyzing their weaknesses and strengths. She wasn't judging, she was learning.

"How did this serve you?" I asked.

"It brought me fulfillment, to see how life evolves. I watched these people grow, grow up, and grow old, but they didn't evolve. They stayed small. They stayed immature and continued to scratch for something outside of themselves. While I stayed grounded with clarity. Knowing that this life of mine was temporary, enabled me to live my life to the fullest. And the only way I was free to live my life as I pleased was by being a few steps ahead of the others. I needed to watch their actions so I could act before they did. I needed to know their words and emotions, so I was free to do as I wished within their strict guidelines. I learned the rules, so I could break them in secret."

The men all moved to the smoking room to discuss political matters, leaving the women to gossip. Margaret was becoming bored with the topic of discussion. The women all gossiped about their peers; who wore what and when. Margaret desired to talk about more worldly ideas, but her duties as a woman prohibited her from doing so.

"You believe you're inferior because they told you so." Margaret pointed to the men as they left the room. "Their power only exists because we all support the laws they made."

Margaret sat in the middle of the sofa in between two women.

"She's crazy!" a woman next to Margaret said, pointing to another woman in the corner.

"Who does she think she is?" said another woman, fluttering her eyelashes and throwing her head back as she laughed.

"She's trying to fight for change for those beneath her, what stupidity!" said another woman, as she took a sip of her glass of wine.

Margaret looked at me and raised her eyebrows, frustrated with her peers.

"See," she said to me. "If it's not me, it's someone else. Everyone needs someone to blame for their own misfortune. We can't do anything in this world without being watched. If the monarchy isn't fining you for stepping out of line, your neighbors will make sure they do. There is nowhere safe anymore. We are all under surveillance."

Margaret looked at me as though waiting for a response. The background faded and all I could see was her outline. Her, in her beautiful red dress covered in laces and beads. This woman magnetized an array of deep emotions within me, yet I felt as though I could see through her. A mirage of prison cells appeared before me, enclosing Margaret like a birdcage, stabilizing her energy.

"I am a woman, and so to them, I am less."

I knew she was referring to the men who judged her. Although women were respected in the era she was living in, it was a selective respect, for the laws all favored men and protected their choices, regardless of how devious they were.

The vision of Margaret in a cage subsided and her dinner guests reappeared, laughing, drinking, and gossiping. Margaret rolled her eyes, signaling her boredom. She pulled me aside, taking me near the windowsill to watch everyone from afar. "I can think and feel whatever I want, but I can't say or do whatever I want. My only power is my opinion, but that opinion is only worth something if another agrees. I am trying everything I can to make changes in the world. I didn't want my children to be raised in this kind of world. But they are, so all I can do is find solutions and support them in secret. I use my own money to support the revolution. I use it to fund the groups that can speak freely and fight for change. I help in any way that I can without being seen. Even if it wasn't the difference I would have liked to have made. I survived the best way I knew how."

Margaret looked out the window at the moonlight, then gazed back at the party. I could feel the looks from the women behind her, watching her. It was not out of admiration for her uniqueness, but from envy.

"Yes, you can feel it too," Margaret smirked. "I need to befriend them or they will call me out like they did to that other woman. A witch isn't just a woman who is punished for witchcraft anymore, it can be anyone who rebels against the agenda of the elite."

I had learned about this truth from many witchcraft history books—that those who were outcast and burned weren't necessarily witches. They were just the women who spoke out against the system. Most often they were Christians who had done something that someone didn't like. So, the easiest way to get rid of your neighbor was to label them as a witch and make it impossible to be proven otherwise. By this point, all true witches were practicing rituals in complete secret, usually on their own. It was impossible to find a real witch; they wouldn't bother to show themselves or their magic in public. They knew that their power needed to be hidden.

"Stay hidden in the world so no one sees you coming, they say," Margaret said, as the vision showed her standing at the door, waving goodbye to her guests. "But I don't want to live a life like that."

The last guest left and Margaret closed the door. The maids were walking around behind her, tidying up the mess. Margaret just stood there, looking at me. A haunting expression on her face—one of both strength and anger. "I am finding solutions," she said, nodding, as though telling herself to keep going. "I will get us out of this."

The haunting image of Margaret standing in front of her grand house was the last I saw of her. There was nothing more to be played out. I felt my own inspiration ignite from within, taking on her determination and thirst for change in the world. Whether Margaret had succeeded in making great changes in the world was irrelevant; the fact that she wanted it was a big enough spark within the collective to create change. She recognized that something was wrong within society and she was seeking how to fix it. Although the problems of inequality are still present in our world today, so many are ignorant of them; therefore complete change can't occur. But Margaret knew what was happening, everywhere, behind closed doors, behind their smiles, behind their words. Margaret knew. She knew because she observed, because she analyzed, and because she questioned their authority. Asking questions would have led to her death had she not been careful. And when I woke up from this journey I found myself embodying the inspiration from Margaret, eager to explore my world with scrutiny to find out how I can create the changes that we need.

Margaret Reflections

I left Margaret's world having understood the lesson that freedom was possible within refined walls. She was a silent feminist. Someone who thought outside from the defined parameters that she had been born into.

Despite there being more than a hundred years between her life and mine, I couldn't help but see that barely anything had changed. She lived in a culture that praised one group and punished the other. Whether it was rich or poor, black or white, female or male, one was always against the other. And the same puppeteers who were holding the strings, were the ones who promoted and enforced fear between the groups, so that peace would never be possible. Because as long as we focused our attention on the opposition, they could grow their power and wealth. And even though we're living in a world that has progressed rapidly over the last century, we are still faced with the same problems, but now with bigger gaps of inequality needing to be bridged. Despite the drastic advances of technology, our freedom is curtailed, due to the constant monitoring of one's actions. If those actions or voices were to go against the narrative that enforced the position of the elite, or if those voices attempted to dismantle the compulsory gender roles that supported the hierarchy, they would be punished. And it wasn't just the governments and their representatives enforcing this, neighbors were also pointing fingers of blame easily too.

Too many people have been brainwashed and made to be afraid, believing they have no power. Those in power want their subjects to believe this lie. They want their subjects to be well-behaved, well-mannered, easily controlled, to gratefully take what is given, and to obey what they are told. But in Margaret's world, I could feel they were no longer buying the narrative that they were given, and the first inkling of change was coming through. She was realizing the truth of what was happening before her and she knew it was wrong.

By this time, the rules of what it meant to be male and female were deeply embedded into their culture. The men were forced to be manly, strong, aggressive, and determined; the women needed to be gentle, submissive, soft, loving, and caring. The men took care of business, made important decisions, and protected their families and property. And the women, their duty was to follow, to support, and abide without question. These roles were created over a thousand years before Margaret's time. And so by now, all the years that had passed had solidified these roles into society. These gender roles have been hammered into our minds since birth, and they are so ingrained into our upbringing that we don't even realize the problem with them. We are so used to societal structure and hierarchy of power that we don't even realize that we also enforce them by accepting them.

When we look closely at the system we will see that it's not only the women who are suffering. For, if a man does not align with the perceived stereotype, he is shunned and ridiculed. There is enormous pressure on the men to behave a particular way and to fit a certain narrative. Many people enjoy playing the stereotype of the masculine and feminine roles; so much so that to mold into each other, or cross over, feels foreign. Many don't know how to handle it. Although we can sympathize with the way the world has been established, we need to realize that we are hindering the happiness of a part of humanity. Therefore it is time this system is dismantled.

It's not just the male who enforces his own power, but the female supports it too. If the masculine steps out from being the pillar of strength for the feminine, the feminine may mock their actions, reminding them of their roles and duties as a man. Our beliefs and reactions are embedded into our culture, enabling the system to continue. Phrases commonly spoken to the masculine by the feminine are on autopilot: "Be strong"; "Don't cry"; "Don't show emotion." We need to allow men to be more vulnerable. We need to allow ourselves to be more open to transformation. In this day and age, we are faced with confusion over what is "masculine" and what is "feminine." When we explore those themes, we need to be sure we are not projecting our own bias upon them. It's important to be open and understand that both energies are present in each of us. Some people may have more of one than the other, and that's okay. It's not good or bad, it simply is. It's not for anyone to judge. We need to remind ourselves that if one of us is hurt, we all are hurt.

Despite the time that has passed between Margaret's life and mine, the problems still exist today. The fight for equality, the suppression of opposing religious beliefs, the discrimination against races, and the gap between the rich and the poor are still alive today. In my waking life, men still dominate the control of the world. They are in possession of the most money and other resources, and they hold the majority of control in politics, making the decisions for all of us. These ideas of what we have grown up to be perceived as normal, are actually purposely placed in order to keep the hierarchy system of power in control. Only in the last hundred years or so have women's rights improved, and even still we are merely scratching the surface. When faced with the questions of society before us, and this need for equality, we need to look at ourselves to see how we are playing our role. It's not enough to support and agree, we need to be acting, recognizing, honoring, and celebrating the beauty of differences between us.

The great reckoning has erupted. The problems are now visible: we recognize that the sovereign no longer serves the people, but has their own agenda. One that promises they stay in power. An agenda that promises the elite to stay wealthy, so that they in turn will stay in power. Church and state may have separated, but the role of the church has now been overtaken by the advances of technology. There is a new player, a new role, a new game. It is one that still controls the people, but instead of using religion as a form of power, they are using news resources, social media, and everyday computer applications. The elite have carefully constructed their marketing campaign to tell you what they want you to know. They are telling you how you have to behave in order to survive. They are telling you half of the story, they are shoving their biases down our throats and we are swallowing it, believing they care for us. Our only solution? To remember our own power and unite together, because there is power in numbers. We need to remember our power within.

Instead of being angry or sad about this terrible truth, we need to turn those emotions into our power. We need to heal our wounds, and turn them into power. The truth needs to be revealed. The inequality needs to be addressed. The world needs to feel the true pain that the less fortunate are enduring. Only by feeling what they feel, by understanding what they went through, and are still going through, can true change occur. Like everything in life that needs to be put right, it comes down to education and understanding. And with these two elements, we can support the younger generation, so that they have the tools to create the changes where we have failed to do so.

No longer will we bow down or suppress our gifts. No longer will we hide who we really are. From now on, I vow to harness my inner power, to use my voice, actions, and every ounce of my being to make things right. I have to, because others died trying to do so. Because if we don't, nothing will change in the next hundred years. And we need to advance in a way that is right. Not in the way that they want us to, but in a way that is best for humanity—with love, compassion, and kindness at the forefront. From this point forward, I will forever remember the witch within.

The Power of Intention

I journeyed through to the upper world and arrived at an old house that sat along the water. When I walked through the door, I discovered an older man. I knew immediately that he was my father in this past life, but he was angry with me. I put my head in my hands and cried, asking him what I had done wrong.

"You aren't visiting, you aren't practicing, you aren't doing," he said.

I knew what he meant. It had been a while since I had visited the spirit world, and I missed it greatly.

The man told me to go upstairs. When I did, I found my mother in her bed, but she was close to dying. My heart began to ache as I felt great suffering, and stress within my mind. I sifted through the pain quickly and smiled at her to give her courage.

"I will never give up. I will use my power to heal you," I said.

The vision before me now played out like a movie, as I watched myself from a bird's-eye view. The vision showed me the duties I performed to help her. I worked constantly, creating rituals to nurture my mother back to health. I watched this version of myself with admiration.

My day began by walking outside in Mother Nature, speaking to her energy, and calling out her name. I asked for her gifts, of healing prayers and her nurturing touch. Her peaceful energy caressed my feet and filled my being with so much love that it overflowed and showered all around me with graceful beauty.

I breathed in deeply and sang as I walked and touched the trees with my hands. The energy of the Earth beneath my feet anchored my soul into my body, grounding my energy, and preparing me for what the day would bring. In this space, I took my time to make peace with the present moment, despite the chaos I felt inside. And I surrendered my fears to the magic of the Universe and trusted the divine power of source creation while doing so.

Next, I gathered fresh flowers from the garden. As I picked each flower, I kissed the ground lovingly, giving gratitude for its beauty and gifts. I set my intention while doing so, asking for Mother Gaia's gift of life to keep blooming for my mother. Sometimes I would cry, and sometimes I would scream with heartache. Sometimes I would allow the overflowing love within me to cocoon me with peace as I gave gratitude for such a brilliant life. And other times, I had sincerity in my vision, knowing, trusting, and believing that my mother would come through, and live vibrantly by my side.

I delivered the fresh flowers to my mother, greeting her merrily with a smile so she couldn't see the pain I felt when seeing her close to dying. I opened the curtains and lifted the windows, inviting pure air and sunlight into the space. As I did so, I said a prayer to this power, thanking it for the breath of life, and asking for its blessings to gift vibrant energy to my mother.

I changed the water by her bedside daily and moved items around in the room to ignite change. This lifted her mood, it changed her energy, as I filled the space with songs of praise and high vibrations. I cooked her nurturing foods to heal her body and spoke affirmations to soothe her soul. At the end of the day, I would light a candle and say another prayer; but, this time, together with my mother. We would speak to the energies of the universe, and ask for a miracle to soothe her soul in this space.

Every morning and night I continued these rituals, constantly sending love, always moving energy, and attempting to raise the vibrations of her soul. Little by little the light in her eyes began to glow. And slowly, bit by bit, her energy changed. I was changing it. I continued with my healing work, using sound to nurture her with love, and harnessing the natural vibrations of the universal energies. Everything was moving. Everything was transforming. I called out to our angels, to our ancestors, and told them she has longer to live with us.

Slowly, the universe listened, and slowly we changed her energy. And in this past life, I learned the most valuable lesson of all—that we have the power to create our reality, to change our reality, and to change the frequencies of the whole world using just our intention.

Released and Me Again

I had a feeling that there were no more lives for me to visit. Still, I journeyed to ask for certainty, and I set up my ritual space with no expectations.

As I arrived at the top of the stairs there was a barrier preventing me from walking forward. The entire platform was surrounded by a cement-like fence, and the king and queen were standing in the center.

"It's finished," the queen announced, confirming my feeling.

I looked at the pathways on the right and left; they were both completely sealed up with cemented barriers.

"And if I need to visit one of the lives again?"

"Then you may do so," she replied. "But you have already done so."

I looked at both of them, smiling with gratitude. "Thank you for your ongoing love and support," I said to them both, as they walked closer to where I was standing. "Thank you so much for your care in helping me reveal the truth of my past." I embraced them both tightly, feeling their love upon me. I knew that I could visit them again if I needed to, but holding that comfort in knowing was all that I needed.

And just like that, I returned to my body. I looked at my hands and feet with familiarity, yet the knowing that it is only temporary still entered my mind. Whenever I wanted to, I knew that I could shake off the layers that make me feel real in this world, and connect once more to the divine light within me. This is where I hold love. This is where I find my peace. Soothing vibrations that hush my fears and I breathe with ease, knowing all is well. I am safe, loved, and protected in my body-like temple.

What did I learn of great significance?

The lives I explored created a great impact on me, one that encouraged deep reflection and intense research of those who came before me. I was shown a whole new layer of understanding and healing needed for the entire conscious collective.

Each life I visited taught me a lesson about power. I could now understand, in greater detail, the power the divine feminine held once upon a time. Their need for survival meant that women needed to deny their powers and the truth of who they really were. Although they thought it would be temporary, that choice to suppress and willingly obey the masculine, carried on for centuries, and still plagues us today. Learning about their pain ignited my own truth, so that I could build confidence within me. I realized that my hesitation to be true to myself, of being a real witch, was because of my history. I realized that I had still been living as though I needed to suppress myself in order to survive. But now we are living in a time of change, of great transformation—"The Great Awakening." In this time, we will remember our power, we will remember our truth, we will stand united and equal. There is a long way to go, but if I can play my small part to encourage that pathway to exist, then I will do so, bravely.

Alfred was the last of my ancestors who truly embodied her power—that of being a witch— unapologetically, and without fear. She taught me to listen to the cravings of my soul, despite the hesitations I may feel. She reminded me about the spirit that resides within every living element in the universe. And that through connecting with those other spirits, we can heal ourselves.

Selina empowered me to believe in the impossible. She was someone who embodied her own divinity in alignment with her soul; she was completely omniscient. Her messages of multiverses and sacred geometry awoke many questions inside my own consciousness, giving birth to new ideas and possibilities. My spiritual practices between my reality and the unseen realms were enhanced because of her guidance. I could feel everything so much more deeply.

Bonita reminds me to never abandon my own power. And that if we ignore the voice of our soul, it will haunt us. I will make sure that I fulfill my needs for survival, and help others meet these too, so that we may be free to soul search and connect with higher powers as we wish. Witnessing Bonita's life enabled me to understand the reasons why she made the choices that she did, and I will apply that same compassion to anyone I may come across whose choices I don't agree with.

Gabriella tells me about the power of our mind, and the importance of aligning with our soul. I am reminded to be grateful for all the opportunities around me, and all the resources I have in today's world. I will not suffer in silence when faced with mental health challenges, as Gabriella did. I will always remind myself of my divine connection with the universe, and seek support as needed.

Georgiana remembered her power, despite being told not to. She listened to the cravings of her soul in secret and managed to live a deeply fulfilling life, despite the challenges she faced of being a woman in her era. She managed to find her guru in the most surprising of people, and she reminds me that anyone can be our teacher. One of the main ways that Georgiana gained her wisdom was through her dreams, and this reminds me of the importance of connecting with the dream world every night that we sleep. We are receiving messages from the spirits in these realms, even if we don't realize it.

Reiko, learned about her power from another. She learned that we must always be open to being the student, knowing that everyone is equal and we are all learning from one another. Reiko's life reminded me of the cycles in the universe, and the rhythmic vibrations of their power. I can now enter a deeper state of meditation because of my experience with her, because of remembering the wisdom that she held.

Margaret reminds me to find my power through self-love. She learned that power can be attained, through knowing yourself, knowing your worth and observing your world. She discovered what it meant to be female, and how to create power even when the system is against you. And the confidence that came with that understanding helped her live freely, despite being constricted in her time of life. She tells me that change is possible, and that every little bit helps.

And, as I reflect upon all of these lives, and see my witchcraft heritage woven ever so slightly throughout them, I understand with greater emphasis why I had held so much fear about owning my gifts. But I will hold no fear anymore. Not just because it would hinder my experience in life, but because those women cannot have died for nothing. Their actions influenced my life today, and I want to make them proud. I need to pave the way for those who come after me. I need to help create a world of equality—by being true to myself, by standing up for what I believe in, and by making sure that everyone is looked after, and that no one is left behind.

Although I am still uncomfortable calling myself a witch, I've decided that I feel more comfortable calling myself a Spiritual Witch. But what is a Spiritual Witch?

A Spiritual Witch follows the path of her higher self. We are connected to our intuition; we honor the divine within ourselves and others equally. We tap into the universal energies surrounding us and harness those energies to benefit our life, all life, with blissful blessings. We create potions (herbal medicines), that heal our bodies. We create rituals that honor our soul and that worship the divinity around us. And in these rituals, we learn how to heal ourselves, how to heal our karmic debt, how to ignite strong inner peace, and how to love the life that we lead.

And so here it is, the end of my book. I hope you enjoyed reading and learning as much as I did. I hope that it has inspired you to unravel your own ancestral and past life history. I hope that it has helped you understand or find comfort in recognizing where your power lies and how you can harness it to create a better future.

The pathway to reveal my greatest self is still unraveling and changing daily. But, I feel more empowered knowing that tapping into the wisdom of the unconscious collective is available to us all, at any time. All we need to do is trust, believe, and continue to practice our sacred rituals, despite the pressures of our outside world. We need to continue to be brave, to speak our truth, to create an equal world for all. And more importantly, we need to listen to each other's stories. We need to support one another, not just the women, but the men too, and allow them to step into a more feminine version of themselves as we step into our own masculine energy. We are a yin and yang of energy circulating together, and we empower one another when we let each other be free to be themselves. All of this and so much more is available at our fingertips. And to harness this power we need to do one simple thing.

We need to remember the witch within.

Books by Phoebe Garnsworthy

Daily Rituals:
Would you like to attract more abundance? More love, more happiness, and more peace? It is available to you right now, if you believe it to be true. Everything in existence is vibrating energy. Whatever you want can be yours if you learn how to emit that vibrational frequency. And from this place, energy will magnetize toward you, naturally connecting like vibrations together. This enables you to attract what it is you wish to seek.

Align with Soul:
In every challenge, we are handed an opportunity to evolve into a better version of ourselves. We are given a choice – either to keep repeating the same mistakes, or to accept the invitation graciously and realize that we have the power within to be our own savior. We can learn how to heal and navigate a fulfilling life path by aligning with our soul to activate the wisdom of the universal love that surrounds us. Learn spiritual philosophy, energy tools, and techniques to inspire your journey toward enlightenment.

Sacred Space Rituals:
This book was created by calling upon ancient spiritual philosophy from around the world. It primarily uses the principles of creative visualization while harnessing the abundance of universal energies that surround you. The purpose of these rituals is to assist you in your journey of personal development and spiritual transformation.

Define Me Divine Me: A Poetic Display of Affection:
In a stream-of-consciousness style fashion we explore the raw truth that provokes our deepest emotions so that we may honor both the light and the dark within us. Together, we allow the words of enlightened wisdom and painful beginnings to wash through us, as we stand back up and claim what is rightfully ours.

and still, the Lotus Flower Blooms:
This spiritual poetry book explores the hardships we face throughout our lives and inspires you to search within to find the tools you need to survive. Like the lotus flower that grows through mud yet rises every day to greet the sunshine without a slither of darkness upon its petals, you will too, move through your life with grace, resilience, and beauty.

Lost Nowhere + Lost Now Here Series:
The Lost Nowhere Book Series explores spiritual witchcraft in a fictional environment. While following the eclectic imagination of a girl called Lily, the reader is taken to another universe, to a magical world called Sa Neo. In this enchanted world you will meet powerful witches, shamans, healers, queens, kings, and mermaids. You will heed their spiritual wisdom, while having all of your senses heightened, as you explore a world of beauty, magic, and miracles.

About the Author

Phoebe Garnsworthy is an Australian female author who seeks to discover magic in everyday life. She travels between the worlds of the seen and unseen, gathering ancient wisdom and angelic energy. Her writings reflect a dance with the mystical and wonderful, an intoxicating love potion to devour in a world that overflows with forgotten love and enchantment. The intention of her writing is to encourage conscious living and unconditional love.

www.PhoebeGarnsworthy.com

Made in the USA
Monee, IL
13 August 2024

63846285R00105